S0-BPO-394

FAMILY EDUCATION CENTRE
22342 SELKIRK AVENUE
MAPLE RIDGE, B.C. V2X 2X5
MAPLE RIDGE

LOVE IN THE BLENDED FAMILY

Step-Families: A Package Deal

Angela Neumann Clubb

MAPLE RIDGE
FAMILY EDUCATION CENTRE
22342 S L   UE,
MAPLE RIDGE, L   X 2X5

Health Communications, Inc.
Deerfield Beach, Florida

Library of Congress Cataloging-in-Publication Data

Clubb, Angela.
   Love in the blended family: step-families: a package deal/by Angela
Neumann Clubb.
   p. cm.
   Includes bibliographical references.
   ISBN 1-55874-135-6
   1. Stepmothers. 2. Remarriage. 3. Parent and child. I. Title.
HQ759.92.C58   1991
306.874 — dc20   90-23157
                                                    CIP

© 1991 Angela Neumann Clubb
ISBN 1-55874-135-6

All rights reserved. Printed in the United States of America. No part
of this publication may be reproduced, stored in a retrieval system or
transmitted in any form or by any means, electronic, mechanical, pho-
tocopying, recording or otherwise without the written permission of
the publisher.

Publisher: Health Communications, Inc.
              3201 S.W. 15th Street
              Deerfield Beach, Florida 33442

Cover design by Iris T. Slones

Dedication

To my parents, Annerose and Kurt Neumann

Also by Angela Neumann Clubb

Wild About Muffins
Mad About Cheddar
Fun in the Kitchen

---

*In Canada: *Mad About Muffins*.

iv

Acknowledgments

I want to acknowledge and give thanks to each member in my blended family (especially Susan, Amy and Chris). And to David, for all the obvious as well as private reasons.

I am also deeply appreciative of my family of friends, old and new, and to Maria Casimirri for what she has given me in loyalty and love.

Thank you also to my sister, Karen Koos, for meeting the typing deadlines of all my books and persevering through several drafts of this one.

My sincere gratitude to the following for their professional input, any effort made on my behalf, and most especially their encouraging words: Betty Jane Wylie, Lynn Johnston, Matie Molinaro, Pat Harris, Elaine Pitre, Bryan Prince, Fred Kerner, Jack McClelland, Drs. Beryl and Noam Chernick and Dr. Axel Russell. Thank you all.

Contents

Introduction

You are reading a book which is deeply meaningful to us both. Whether you are a stepfamily initiate or a veteran, have passive or active involvement, you and I have something in common: our desire for meaningful relationships and love within the blended family circle.

Love in the Blended Family is my very biased look at stepfamilies, particularly the role of stepmother and second wife. I do not wish to presume that I fully know or understand how my husband David, his ex-wife Heather, my children Adam and Annie, or my stepchildren Elizabeth and Robert, view our family life. For this reason, I largely placed the magnifying glass on myself and my experiences as they relate to key issues common to most stepfamilies. My hope is that aspects of your own family life will be mirrored back to you. More essentially perhaps, you may be able to relate to some of the conflicting emotions which I needed to understand and acknowledge. In many ways, stepfamilies live on an inner and outer level, a sort of "dual life" which requires not only a good deal of energy but also emotional resiliency. Almost from the beginning, David and I fluctuated between the couple-oriented world of two lovers and the child-oriented world of two part-time parents. Though we didn't intend it that way, once we had our own children, everything became more chaotic and complex. Thus his children, our children, his ex-wife and her family, his family and my parental family, all became parts of our "blended family"; each member needing to find a comfortable place in the family circle.

The term *blended family* has been aptly coined for the reason that a stepfamily tries so much to look and act as normal as possible. Although the appearance of an instant family may be there, looking and feeling normal is a monumental task. New ties are often formed before family members have worked through the processes of loss and separation and acknowledged a host of feelings. Ultimately, however, each of us begins our journey to achieve a sense of unity within our new *package deal:* our blended family.

But the package is fragile and certainly not perfect. It's a volatile little package, but very private and self-contained nonetheless. To the world at large, it wants to look solid and together, anything less would seem like failure.

It is this facade of always "looking OK," (a facade I internalized) which motivated *Love in the Blended Family.* Even as the book was finished, I experienced new problems. I would barely finish a chapter, when another would suggest itself. And any smugness I might have momentarily felt about the kind of second wife, mother or stepmother I thought I was, was soon replaced with a good deal of anxiety and humility as new lessons came my way.

Reality (particularly something as close to home as family reality) needs to be expressed. As blended families don't go for counseling often enough, and live interspersed in communities which are still making adjustment to the growing number of single-parent households as well as stepfamilies, it is my hope that this book will serve to portray one family with whom you may share common concerns and dreams.

Angela Neumann Clubb

Prologue

Angela unlocked the apartment door. Two steps behind, David followed, carrying a massive role of carpet with less effort than one would think was possible. Hesitating momentarily, he maneuvered himself to the far wall, dropped the roll and busied himself on his knees.

This is nice. He's going to place it for me, too.

Casually flinging her purse aside on the hardwood, Angela disappeared into the kitchen.

"I can't tell you how much I appreciate this!" she called out. "When I bought the carpet from Pat, I wondered how I would ever manage. Despite the fact that you're her *only* friend with a station wagon, are you always this helpful?"

Emerging from the kitchen with a bottle of beer, Angela came toward him. David looked up with a quick smile, wondering what he could possibly say to sound more impressive than the two-word answers he'd been giving her all evening.

"Glad to be able to help," he said, taking the beer.

Talk about the strong silent type!

With a scrutinizing glance, Angela flopped herself directly across from him, resting her back against the wall.

"Let's relax and take a break — you must be beat!" Realizing he had no intention of starting a conversation, she quickly asked, "How long have you known Pat and Gary?"

"A few years now. Gary and I fish together."

God, this is like pulling teeth!

With her voice deliberately casual, Angela continued.

"And Pat tells me that you're almost divorced, David?"

"Yes, I've been on my own for two years now . . . It's working out all right. My kids stay with me for a day . . ."

Darn, he's got kids! That's the last thing I need in my life right now. I wonder if they're brats?

"How old are your kids, David?"

Whether surprised by her unexpected question, or having temporarily drawn a blank on his children's ages, he took a moment to answer.

This is obviously a man who thinks before he opens his mouth.

"My kids are young; my daughter Elizabeth is four and my son Robert is three."

Oh, no. What a lot of work!

"I can imagine they must be close!" Angela responded, smiling engagingly. "And do you find that visits with them work out well with your ex?"

I wonder if she's one of the hostile or the friendly ones?

"Yup, my arrangements with Heather are on a pretty friendly basis. I can see the kids whenever I like."

She probably calls him for every household crisis!

"And has Heather found someone else?"

David shifted his position.

"Heather has a friend, but it doesn't appear they'll be getting married," he answered matter-of-factly.

"I see."

All right, so he can talk after all, but his shirt is so frayed. He's probably paying out a fortune. He's already got two kids, why would he want more? Even if he did, he likely can't afford it. His kids are so young; who left whom? You've just spent four years playing stepmother!

Angela wondered if she was fated for stepmotherhood. There was no getting around it. David Clubb would be "a package deal."

PART I:

When Everything Old Is New Again

The Second Wife

Having been a second wife
Not just once
But indeed twice
I have an outlook
On the issue
That could waste
A box of tissue.

In considering
"the plunge"
Think of this
Before you lunge:

It's hard to be a second wife
When the first wears
Joy perfume

And his friends still lose their breath
Each time
She steps into a room
They say
She's a young version
Of the lovely Princess Grace
For she's blessed with classic beauty
Suiting pearls
And heirloom lace

Idolized by his own brother
Much admired by his mother
Groomed and perfumed to her toes
Stunning
In designer clothes
With an enviable career
(They promoted her last year)

What does she really think of me
It shall remain a mystery
Real feelings are suppressed
By pride
We're absolutely civilized
So much so that
It does not please me
To think we've made it look
So easy!

(I wonder if it's not too late
To cultivate a healthy hate?)

How smug to be a second wife
When that which you so dread
Turns out to be quite human
With a little midriff spread
How easy
To be gracious
When you don't feel second rate
And his family tells you frankly that
"The first one" wasn't great

Well,
"They'd known it all along
She'd been absolutely wrong!"

After a lengthy verbal beating
My new in-laws were
Appalled
When I announced quite flatly
That I liked her
After all.

Angela Neumann Clubb

1

Dreams And Reality

*There is only so much you can learn about
skydiving from standing on the ground.*

Joyce Maynard

David was a typical, non-custodial weekend father. It's
not difficult to spot one on a Sunday in any city park. He's
the man trying a little too hard to "play," but his face gives
him away — a mixture of joy, melancholia and awkwardness. David's children were pre-schoolers when his marriage ended, and by the time I met them they were happily
familiar with, and surprisingly resilient to, their back-
and-forth visits to Dad's place. Within weeks of our relationship, I easily stepped into the role of "Daddy's friend,
Angie," and had very little trouble winning them over,
particularly as I was so eager to put a great deal of energy
into our day-trips. I made that sound easy, didn't I?

Yes, I thought it was. I was childless, with lots of after-
hour time to play. With a 30th birthday looming in the
not-too-distant future, childbirth was preoccupying my
thoughts a lot in those days. As my relationship with
David became more serious, I reasoned that I was fated

for package deals. I had more than enough experience for the job, having stepped out of a long-term relationship with similar circumstances a year before.

Adding our own children to a situation I had already handled well in the past seemed no big issue to me (at least not in the monumental terms my parents were thinking). If reading a story to a stepchild had been fun for me in the past, I reasoned, just think of the pleasure it would bring with my own full-time child; taking him or her to baby-and-mom swimming classes, grinding cooked carrots in one of those little health-food grinders, and choosing baby wallpaper. This marriage was really going to work. I could feel it!

Here it was my turn to be "typical": a woman who was placing her hopes on a new relationship, while still trying to put the memories of a disillusioning one behind. This time, I was convinced that David and I could build a relationship in which not only our dreams, but also our reality, would be in harmony.

The difficulty in aligning our dreams with reality becomes easier to grasp once we think about the process of endings and new beginnings. Those of us who begin new relationships, having just come out of another, understandably yearn for feelings of hope and renewal. We become dreamers once again and romantically focus our thoughts on what life could, and would, be like with a new love, with new circumstances, a new lifestyle and family.

And why not? Each of us needs to dream. Without dreams, we seem to ourselves to be only half alive — numb and lacking enthusiasm. Beginning anew is a frightening, as well as an exhilarating experience. Feelings surface as in childhood or adolescence, when everything was a drama, everything had potential and every dream was possible!

I had been here before, difficult dreams with different realities, and yet always I came back to the same $50,000 question. Should I dream and risk, or live safely with less emotional expenditure? I did not want to accept or admit that my life could not be as I imagined it.

The reality is, however, that when I married David, I once again became a member of a blended family, each member of which had his own personal dream, existing quite apart from mine, or those shared by the family. As I began to live within my newly reconstituted family circle, I discoverd that my dreams would gradually have to readjust themselves or become lost altogether. It was during this process of continually working at my relationships that I was compelled to grow, and through which I learned the meaning of the word "commitment." In this marriage I would also learn to come to terms with my personal dreams of motherhood, as well as stepmotherhood, neither of which seemed to be living up to what I felt were my real-life efforts.

I have since concluded that my answer to that $50,000 question lies in the energy we put out to find a balance between being both dreamer and realist. Successful living in a blended family — any family — is a juggling act in which one must learn to hold on to some very personal dreams, all the while trying to deal with the very real obstacles that seem to stand in their way. It's much like being a caterpillar and butterfly at the same time.

If divorce restructures the family so that it becomes a receptacle of lost dreams and disillusionments, little wonder that we have such a tremendous need to experience renewed hope and to feel again our potential for real happiness in remarriage. And that's just the adults!

Many of us have children in tow, similarly disillusioned and with deep needs for reassurance. It becomes easy to understand then that children have been known to cling to what is referred to as a *reconciliation fantasy*. And surprisingly, it does not seem to matter all that much how old these children are when their parents separate. Most children secretly harbor a wish for their parents to reconcile. And this secret wish should not be taken lightly. It possibly becomes so real for them that they carry it over, long after their parents have remarried. David and I had already been married several years when Elizabeth confided that she envied the friends at school who had "regular" moms and dads. She often wished for the same family life, without visitations, with David and Heather at home together.

Creating New Traditions And History

Some couples, in trying to ease the pain for the child, go to unending lengths to keep holidays, birthdays and other family celebrations just as they were prior to separation. This loving gesture can, however, create an awkward and painful situation for the separating adults, and it has been suggested that it actually feeds the reconciliation fantasy within the child. Furthermore, I believe it may even feed a secret wish for reconciliation in the adult who may not have fully desired or accepted the separation.

Traditions are so valuable, for they contribute to the sense of security which all family members, and especially children, must have. The better alternative for a new blended family is to establish some new traditions, giving the restructured family fresh beginnings and a new sense of history. Festivities as well as small rituals can be looked forward to if you are not trying to duplicate that which was once meaningful with other individuals.

As always, such advice is wonderful in theory but will likely meet with resistance by at least some in the family, particularly the children. Even in a nuclear, non-blended family, deviation from the norm or status-quo is often met with resistance.

Picture this: Mother, having gone to a great deal of effort to make an exotic new stuffing for the Christmas bird, hears only complaints such as . . . "This isn't our real stuffing, Mom!" Imagine then, Mother and Dad are separated and these same children now find themselves visiting Dad in his new home. He is now living with a new woman who does many things differently from Mom. Worse yet, even Dad has changed some of his habits to accommodate his new lifestyle! In *Divorce Without Victims*, Stuart Berger points out that this rigidity in children to accept anything different from the norm is one of the most difficult things a stepparent must learn to deal with.

It's a tough situation all around. A new stepmother may feel she is under a critical eye no matter what she does.

The worst part of this, for me, was knowing that as an adult I should be more mature than the children. On an objective level, I could understand the children's reactions. On a feeling level, I often found myself overly sensitive. It was an effort not to take it personally when one of them didn't respond to something I thought was great.

To keep in mind that it is not a dislike of you, but simply a need to hang on to the way things "used to be," is one of the most difficult things any stepparent must learn to deal with. The resistance is simply the way any child may express his huge need for security. Come to think of it, I know many adults who fight change in much the same way for the same reasons.

So Dad's new companion may decorate the Christmas tree in blue and silver, when before it was always multicolored. And her potatoes may be stomped, not whipped like Mom's. Dad himself may introduce something new, and if they like it, he can re-introduce it another time, thus making a small tradition of it. No question that life has changed for the children, but in its place there will be new traditions and, more importantly, new consistencies that they can depend on.

In our family there were a number of things we started years ago, which became traditional activities at Dad and Angie's. This means that when Elizabeth and Robert arrive on Friday evening, they are likely to enjoy popcorn and television to start the weekend off, and on Saturday mornings it's the usual breakfast specialty — Dad's no-recipe corn pancakes. And just about when I think we should be offering them something new for a change (thinking they must be getting bored with popcorn and pancakes), one of them (including Adam and Annie) will pipe up with "Pancakes tomorrow, right, Dad?" I sense their pleasure in this small ritual. I also know that if I were to make the pancakes on Saturdays, they wouldn't taste as good at all! That's when I have to bear in mind that choosing Dad's pancakes over mine has more to do with that comfortable feeling of predictability all children need, than my pancake-making expertise. Furthermore, it allows David to not only demonstrate his affection toward the children in a nonphysical way, but feel appreciated as well. This can be a particularly positive thing in households where children receive few physical signs of parental love.

David's children and I quite naturally came to discover similar small rituals, instigated by me, and shared by all of us. When I discovered that their mother, Heather, disliked spaghetti, and Elizabeth and Robert were wild about it, I jokingly announced we would have an "Italian weekend" in which we ate nothing but, from the moment they arrived Friday evening until Sunday. While they delighted in overdosing themselves on tomato and pasta variations, it established itself as a ritual by repetition and became one of the children's best early memories of weekends with Angie and Dad.

Feelings Of Failure

While some of us are dealing with the small sensitive issues of incorporating new traditions into the blended family, there are yet larger issues to think about, including our sense of failure in not having made it happily through the first marriage. As common as it is now, divorce is still viewed by many as a personal failure. Women, especially, have been conditioned to think that "they" must do everything to make their marriage work, although men are just as vulnerable to these feelings.

Just as women have idealized marriage, so have some men also viewed a good marriage as an extension of their success in the world. It is well known that corporate men are frowned upon when they divorce, as it appears to be a reflection of failure in the home front.

Dragging along this kind of emotional baggage with its perceived sense of failure happened to my friend, Barbara, who otherwise could only have been proud of her past. I became aware of her feelings by chance (she would have been the last person I thought harbored feelings of failure). I can only wonder now how many other genuinely nice, as well as accomplished, people retain this judgment of themselves because they choose not to stay with a former mate. Outwardly, she will always *appear* to have the ideal life: beautiful home, dynamic children, successful husband. Inwardly, she had it all too: a loving nature, an artistic gift, intelligence and more. Yet, her husband was self-absorbed and uncommunicative and she felt deeply unhappy in this, her second marriage. When she confided that the situation had little chance of bettering itself, I responded, empathetically with, "Perhaps you should consider leaving?" It was then that she looked at me aghast, as if I were suddenly her estranged mate. Obviously, to her, I had missed one very crucial understanding. "I would never do that!" she protested. "And fail twice!"

Despite the fact that Barbara had outgrown her marriage or may have needed more love than her husband was prepared to give, it was trivial next to the massive sense of failure she would feel if she were to leave.

I realize now that my friend still operated under some very unyielding values, typical of our parents' era. Values with the message, "You've made your bed, now lie in it," or "When you buy a ticket, you see the show." David, who very much comes from this kind of conservatism, has been known to come out with the latter expression, and it always gets my back up. It is in those moments that I remind myself that one of the things I value about him is his sense of discipline, and ability to work his way doggedly through a task or commitment to its completion. The values of our parents' generation are very good for us as long as they are not applied to our life as inflexible black/ white rules to live by, no matter what. Rigidity in any area of thought is negative and can become a force destructive to personal happiness. As with most things, there is a need for balance in our attitudes.

In my friend's case, Barbara had rebelled once already against her conservative upbringing when she left her first husband. The price had been too high for her and

she had suffered mental anguish over her family's disapproval. Having pieced her life together, at least outwardly,
she was living her dream and Barbara could not afford to
go back. It simply represented failure — again.

Feelings of failure, then, lie at the root of most stepfamilies. In divorce situations which involve children,
recriminations and a sense of failure can rarely be
avoided. The first hurdle is to convince the children that
they are not failures, nor are they in any way responsible
for the separation. Most likely, on some level, parents
feel responsible for placing their children in a painful
situation, as well as failing to provide them hereafter
with a "normal" family life.

For the single parent with whom the child lives, there is
the potential for a "double whammy." This parent may
experience feelings of failure on two counts: denying the
child a normal family life, and fear of doing an inadequate
parenting job as the custodial parent. Excluding the co-
parenting situation, a custodial parent usually feels emotionally burdened, knowing that for the most part, he/she
now has sole responsibility. To yearn for new beginnings,
where these responsibilities are once again shared, is easy
to understand. It is also problematic: on the one hand, the
prospect of another marriage creates feelings of romance
and hope; on the other, if the separation has instilled a
deep sense of failure, the fear of history repeating itself
attracts negativity from the onset.

Unfortunately, the reassurance that many adults are looking for when embarking on a new relationship with potential permanence is "instant togetherness" and "instant fun."
The process of rebuilding new family ties is a slow one for
the separating parents. They must first deal with their
tendencies to use denials and false reassurances with their
children. In reality, they are putting their children through
some degree of pain, and this pain needs to be expressed
openly rather than masked with false words. As difficult
as this may be, it often creates a new and deeper emotional
closeness between parent and child, which in part compensates for some of the negativity experienced.

Let us dismiss then from our thinking the worn-out term "failed marriage" when hereafter referring to a "former marriage." If this is difficult to do, then perhaps it is a good idea to consider doing what Nancy Baker calls, in her book *New Lives for Former Wives*, a psychological autopsy on the marriage. By this, Baker suggests we should accept the notion that a relationship which once worked for us simply doesn't any longer, or possibly we just "outgrew" it. Baker comes to this point of view through her reasoning that women come to marriage with a number of expectations given to them by their parents. Our parents, after all, were probably our role models as children, and we, as witnesses to their marriage, similarly tried to live out these roles when we took a partner.

The positive aspect of maturing is that we change and develop in new directions. These directions, however, don't always parallel those of our parents, and as much as we may have made positive change in our lives, we also may have outgrown the roles we adopted from them.

The Marriage Myth

Many of our romantic ideals were also adopted from our parents. The ideals we associate with marriage are what have created *the marriage myth:* a coined term, to describe our desire to view marriage as "forever" and "all-encompassing." Furthermore, we have been conditioned to believe that we should be able to expect everything from our partner and marriage: love, companionship, passion, and intellectual stimulation.

Not long ago, a survey concluded that young teenage girls are especially susceptible to the myth; dreaming of having picture-book children with Tom Selleck-type mates, who will provide them with a dream-home (fireplace et al.) in which the couple spends many romantic hours sharing long talks.

Our need to cling to this ideal is evidenced by the booming sales of romance novels and the romantic dramas fed to us by movies and television. My middle-aged friend

Beth acknowledges privately that her marriage is mediocre, but her dreams thrive on daily rations of Harlequin romances. As such, light romantic fantasies can be a healthy escape when we need to dilute the stresses of daily living. When they become an addictive dependency, as with Beth, who has difficulty tolerating her life without her books, something is clearly out of whack. Beth, like many women, has chosen to stay in a dissatisfying but predictable relationship, rather than risk the revival of her dreams by acting on them and leaving her relationship.

In contrast to Beth is the newly-separated man or woman, hoping to shift the tide from disillusionment to long-awaited marital happiness. But how? The dream must be tempered not only with our personal energy, but also patience and time.

Unfinished Business And Unhooking

One thing we especially need to give ourselves time for is the mental process of disengaging from our former relationship. We must internalize the reality that we are no longer living with our spouse and really come to terms with the disillusionments of our marriage (on a gut/feeling level), that is, accept the fact that we need to move out not only physically, but also emotionally. Research indicates that this *unhooking process*, as it is called, takes equally as long as the marital bonding process, which is approximately two years. It is realistic then to give ourselves at least one year to detach on various internal levels from our former mates.

The joke about the husband who went out to buy a bottle of milk and never came back represents for me the kind of intense inner abandonment one experiences when suddenly faced with carrying on alone. One may realize quite physically that a mate is gone, but the emotional unhooking process is painfully long. The process can be compared to the feelings which surface after someone close to us has died: disbelief, hurt, guilt, anger, hope, depression, and finally acceptance. For children, the final phase of resolution and acceptance is attained with utmost difficulty, and it may be that a child never completely unhooks. As for adults, Grant Berke, author of *Games Divorced People Play*, maintains that a good indication of having unhooked from a former mate is when you can see or interact with that person without feeling badly.

I personally acknowledge that it took me much longer to unhook, even though my life was long since fulfilled and busy with activities involving my new marriage. It was five years before I was able to listen to songs which had come to hold special significance for me during my relationship with Paul without feeling a wave of nostalgic sadness.

Resolving residual feelings toward one's ex falls under the area of *unfinished business*. I very much like this term because it so clearly describes all things pending, emotional or otherwise. Only after we have dealt with unfinished business can we move on to something new. Sadly though, many couples do form new relationships while they still have unfinished business to tend to. Yet it would be unrealistic, as well as unfair, to recommend that separated couples put their love interests "on hold" while giving themselves the two to three years to emotionally move away from a former spouse. For those couples who have formed a blended family and still have unfinished business to resolve, it is likely that the children will view the stepparent as a disruptive factor regardless of whether that person contributed to the actual marriage breakdown. And if those children coexist in an "instant" blended family, the children will likely be responsible in part for the hostile atmosphere in the home.

Establishing a friendly way of dealing with one's ex over sensitive issues like money and visitation rights further complicates life. After all, this was someone we once loved, someone we allowed ourselves to be vulnerable with. With the memory of past hurts still fresh, rather than taking an empathetic stance many couples are really trying to convey the message, "Look at me. My life is better without you. I am in control." The less unfinished business we have, the less chance for this kind of defensive posture, and the better chance we have to make our new relationships work.

On that score, David and I were very fortunate. When we first met, he had been separated for over two years and had long since worked out a friendly arrangement for access, as well as settling unfinished emotional issues.

As far as I could see, there appeared to be no residual anger, feelings of betrayal or marital sour grapes of any kind. As with few other separated men I had met, David had no obsessive need to list any faults and hurts Heather might have inflicted. The danger in doing this sort of inventory is that new loves unconsciously begin the cycle of comparing every facet of themselves to their former spouse.

How lucky for me! Heather had also come to terms with any grievances she may have had about her former marriage. There was a high degree of cooperation toward me from the start. Frankly, I couldn't believe it at first. Too good to be true, I thought. Heather had her own interests, social life, church, ceramic classes, and the support of her immediate family. She clearly did not view herself as a personal failure; it made dealing with her much easier and more agreeable.

Fears

So that left me to face some of my own fears. Though unaware of it then, I have since come to realize that these fears are typically experienced by many second wives, as well as second husbands.

Some of these fears were: What did David and I have to give to each other at all? What was new and refreshing? Something previously not shared with the former mate? Would it be my appreciation for Brandenburg Concertos or my passion for smoked fish? My friend Wanda, for example, was personally delighted to introduce her new love to the wonderful art of picnicking, and this new pastime came to hold much ritual and significance for them.

In numerous irrelevant ways, David, too, compared himself to my former companion Paul and needed the reassurance that I appreciated him for what he, and no one else, could bring to our relationship.

I wonder how many second wives have outdone themselves in the area of gourmet cooking only after hearing that the former wife could barely defrost in the microwave? Are women more prone to comparisons than men? Whatever else research might conclude, it is my personal bias that sex is one area where both partners must ultimately feel secure with one another. Do I measure up romantically? And do I really want to hear about it?

Of course we do! But no descriptive details please! A man or woman who talks about their ex-mate in terms of "how much sex, how intensely satisfying," runs the risk of lodging potentially destructive impressions in the mind of a new partner. What is reassuring, however, is to know that there is no residual attraction left for him or her, particularly if one is obliged to maintain a cooperative relationship with a former spouse.

Falling in love again, saying the words, and making the promises — that was the easy part. Optimist that I am, I thought I had fallen in love with a package more perfect than anyone would dare hope for and feared no great obstacles ahead. I did not understand that I was dealing with a number of individuals who would affect me directly and subtly. David's and my decision to marry had the same far-reaching reaction as throwing a stone into a pond. Positive as well as negative vibrations would come back to us from all directions. Our private world came to include his parents, mine, mutual friends, his ex and the ghost of mine.

Laying A Good Foundation

Despite the fact that we may have entered marriage with a number of naive expectations, one would hope that the reasons for marrying in the first place were sound. According to some professionals, laying a good foundation is of prime importance for successful living within the blended family. Couples are seriously advised to marry for the right reasons. Loneliness, insecurity, or sexual attraction are simply not good enough, although I know plenty of people who have united on just those grounds.

Before embarking on a second marriage, Tom Frydenger, author of *The Blended Family*, himself a stepparent as well as a family counselor, offers the following advice:

1. Have a lengthy courting period.
2. Allow future stepchildren to fully see your shortcomings.
3. As adults, exchange explicit goals and come to a mutual understanding of each other's expectations.
4. Don't exaggerate your future mate's qualities to your children.
5. Clearly verbalize to the children how they fit into the new stepfamily.

In all cases, there are exceptions. Although laying a good foundation may be a desirable thing to do, it does not mean that a marriage is doomed if it is entered into spontaneously, with none of the cautious pre-planning that Frydenger recommends. David and I are a case in point. We made a commitment to one another very early in the relationship, and it has lasted.

Attitudes: Parents And In-Laws

To begin with, both sets of parents had little time to adjust, considering our brief courtship. Secondly, they were like night and day. In my family, we all lived in each other's pockets, a close-knit European household. And did they worry, worry, worry! Their love was biased and protective, and initially they viewed David as yet another man, who brought all kinds of complicated circumstances. The idea of cooperative blended families was something they could barely cope with, as none of their friends had ever divorced. This being the case, my mother could not fathom why I was not jealous of Heather. How could I stand him seeing her every few weeks to pick up the children? And it was just too, too puzzling for her when Heather started to send plates of Christmas cookies my way via David!

When we brought Elizabeth and Robert around to visit, my parents were wonderful with them, always welcoming them into their home. They thought perhaps that David expected them to love Elizabeth and Robert, but it wasn't the same as if they had been my children. We didn't expect it to be.

When Adam and Annie came along, my parents gushed and fussed over them. Clearly they felt more strongly about my children than David's, and their awareness of this created some awkwardness for them. When Elizabeth and Robert were present, my mother, who shows her feelings easily, would over-compensate to make the older kids and David feel good. Sometimes it was all a bit much at my house.

David's folks, on the other hand, were the model of controlled conservatism, detachment — your basic "untouchables." That was the most difficult thing for me to handle, as Paul's mother had been extremely demonstrative. After recovering from that shock, I soon realized a number of other crucial differences. One of my earliest memories was a discussion in which I shared with David's mother my possible plans to delay pregnancy so that I might enter law school. "David loves his home life, and you're over-educated already" was her response. It was incomprehensible to me that she considered university education for women superfluous. My future mother-in-law's tone was loaded with disapproval. I was also aware that David's parents had built a relationship with Heather, and as sewing and needlepoint happened to be one of her talents, Heather clearly had more to share with David's mother than I.

Well, I didn't go to law school, and I acquired a potter's wheel instead of a sewing machine. What saved me in her eyes, I'm sure, was that I did end up staying home with my children, and I loved to cook. Nevertheless, I was acutely aware of the fact that she appeared to have much more in common with Heather than me, and quite obviously looked forward to chats with Heather when she brought Elizabeth and Robert around.

Should I have been jealous or defensive or sad? I was at times all of these. Comparisons were not so much talked about but made, nonetheless, and on occasion I found myself back in the bathtub, having inner monologues with that insecure persona . . . the second wife.

2

Cooperation And Competition

No bed is big enough to hold three.

German Proverb

We've all made comparisons between ourselves and the people in our lives, and whether we like to do it or not, we have been conditioned to compete on many levels since childhood. No family is exempt from this — it's what soap opera writers thrive on. Mothers and daughters, sisters, lovers; these relationships are all subject to competition. My personal feeling is that any two women who have cohabited with or loved the same man, have on some inner level, made comparisons and experienced feelings of competition.

Prior to meeting David's ex-wife Heather for the first time, I had a vivid memory of encounters with my former companion's ex-wife Linda. Before Linda would allow Paul weekend visitations with their son Brendon, she requested to meet with me, in order to determine whether I would be a good influence on her child. What could I say? (It's amazing what a woman in love will subject herself to.) I agreed to the "interview."

21

Nervous as a cat, but hoping Paul would think I was casual about it, I was more than a little unnerved when she opened her front door and I found myself face-to-face with a Grace Kelly replica! . . . And all this time Paul had been telling me that she wasn't beautiful in his eyes. Really Paul! How could I ever believe you again?

Without exaggeration, this woman possessed the kind of "peaches and cream" classic beauty that I would have killed for in my high school years. "Have you done much baby-sitting?" she asked. "Have you ever been a camp counselor?" she queried this "country mouse." That was my first exposure to "Grace," and her aura continued to fascinate me during the next four years as she would greet me with detached friendliness when Paul and I arrived every second weekend to pick up Brendon. I could have stayed home, you might say? True, but I was into sharing everything in those days.

Despite the fact that I felt I had allowed myself to be interviewed in the name of "Brendon's welfare," it was also clear to me then, that while Linda asked her questions, with Paul quietly sitting beside me witnessing our exchange, the atmosphere was loaded with private emotions and motives I could only guess at. I understand now that neither of them had been given adequate time to unhook which left unfinished business to resolve between them during the years I was with Paul. Since my own initiation into motherhood, I can also understand that it was important for her to meet me as she was entrusting her son partially into my care for a weekend.

Not so with Heather. What a relief to meet a woman with a nice assortment of great and not-so-great features. Right from her first hello, this ex-wife seemed genuine, cooperative and nice (too nice). As a matter of fact, her goodwill was a little overwhelming. Still, I was pleased and determined to show my maturity. Why shouldn't two women be able to relate in an easy-going manner and put comparisons aside? How nice, I thought, that this time around I wasn't conscious of lacking career credentials (Linda had been a corporate manager). How nice, I thought, that I was eyeball-to-eyeball with a five foot one inch woman who didn't have Barbie doll legs on a five foot nine inch frame.

The Cooperation/Competition Conflict

Psychologist Theodore Isaac Rubin in his book *One on One*, refers to this as the *cooperation/competition conflict*. Rubin feels that competition is a natural human trap we fall into. On the one hand, we desire to compare and compete; on the other, there is an equal and genuine willingness to cooperate. I'll admit to his claim that this creates a feeling of inner anxiety, one which can build up over time. As well, it contributes to many of the double messages we sometimes send out.

The natural cooperation/competition conflict is just as evident in children. *Sibling rivalry* is simply another term for it, and parents often fuel this unknowingly when they send the mixed message: be competitive, but get along. Concerning children, two areas of conflict which come to mind immediately are the strong feelings of ownership children have toward their possessions, and the skills and talents which they have developed. David and I have always discouraged the children from competing with one another. As is natural, however, children will compare on a simple level who received what for Christmas, for example. And because the older children only shared in our weekend time, new acquisitions were also noted — a new print on the wall, a car for Angie, or a new bike for Adam.

Occasionally, however, there are comparisons made that a parent can do little about, as during the period when Adam at age five was almost the same height as Robert, then age ten. Due to body structure and heredity, it became evident that Adam would develop into a big boy. Robert was already conscious of his smallness, but his gutsy nature easily made up for this. Adam, however, could not understand why, at five, he could not ride a two-wheeler just like Robert, swim like Robert, and do many of the things he admired in his older stepbrother.

David and I felt sympathy for Adam as he tried to compete and continually felt himself to be lacking. Adam's inability to grasp that he shouldn't expect to accomplish what Robert could, just because they looked almost equal in size, bothered me enormously. But eventually, that phase passed too as Robert had a growth spurt and Adam slowly acquired some of the skills he wanted to master so badly.

Take the stresses that rivalry brings to a conventional household, magnify them many times over, and you will come close to understanding the potential resentments which can arise between blended family households.

Picture: Allan has just married Sara. It is Sara's first marriage. Sara has always been very jealous not only of the time Allan spends with the kids, but also of the discussions he's had with his ex regarding their schooling. When they do come for the day, Sara often finds herself tense, but reasons that as soon as she has a child of her own, she will be able to teach her child everything that her stepchildren are rejecting. No sooner is the baby born than Sara becomes even more demanding with Allan and considers his children an intrusion on their threesome. To make matters worse, Sara becomes even more critical of her stepchildren as she fears their behavior will influence her baby negatively. Allan now finds himself in a no-win situation: he loves them all! The pressure he feels from Sara contributes to the quarrels which by now are affecting the entire reconstituted circle.

This unhappy example is not meant to point the accusatory finger at Sara, who may well have had her own legitimate grievances as stepmother, and her own difficult adjustments to make. The illustration was meant to highlight two factors: first, Sara's competitive nature is her worst enemy in this situation and second, as the second wife, she has a good deal of power in setting the emotional climate in her household. However, her cooperation/competition conflict alienates the very people with whom she wishes to live in harmony.

If this description of blended family living seems to imply that family members fall into roles of either "victims" or "tyrants," allow me to qualify this somewhat, by pointing out that likely each of us has, at one time or another, played both roles in our relationships. Depending on the circumstance, have you manipulated or been manipulated in the past? Children, too, are adept at making us feel they are victims (just at the moment they are tyrannizing us as parents). How we allow ourselves to fall into these roles is another matter, but as one adult relating to another, I am aware that whenever I have felt myself a victim, on some level I have given consent to the process. Similarly, when I analyze the times I have been a witch, someone else, too, has allowed that to happen.

I feel that a child, who is manipulated by two competitive parents who destructively compete for that child's affection and loyalty, is a true victim of a pathetic circumstance. This is particularly sad to witness within blended families. Unfortunately it does not exist solely between two biological parents: a new stepfather will often compete with the non-custodial, biological father; a mother may turn her children against their new stepmother; even grandparents vie for a child's attention by discrediting one another. Such power struggles do not have the child's interest at heart; at the very least they are indications of serious unfinished business.

Friendly Ex-Husbands And Ex-Wives

Really competitive struggles, such as these, have never become a part of my own blended family life. I was quite content to remain "Angie" and had no real wish to replace Heather in her children's hearts. I will, however, confess to some competitive vanity in two areas of my life: first, my personal image and second, my good cooking. So, when Heather sent us her Christmas cranberry loaf, did you really think that I was going to give it the taste-test and compare it to my own? On all points related to food, you may label me "Goldilocks" who found "Mama Heather-bear's" too sweet or too sour — and, of course, mine just right! As for my image? What second wife, in her right mind, wouldn't want to look great in the presence of her man's ex-wife? For that matter, what second wife wouldn't wish to wow her ex-husband (just to rub in what he's been missing all these years)?

Which is why I must share with you the one and only recent time I encountered my first husband, Ted, with whom I had shared a very early two-year student marriage at university.

The last time we had seen each other was eight years previously when I had been in one of those rare peak periods in my life in terms of body image, feeling and looking great! On this day, however, all 180 pounds of me, pregnant, was rushing around doing errands in preparation for my second child, due in less than one month. It was that dreary, cold, wet time in March and because I did not have a proper overcoat, I decided to grab a bulky, age-old tweed jacket I'd worn in my college days. As I was struggling to maneuver myself into the car, I was jolted to awareness by someone calling, "Angie . . . Angie," from across the road. Looking up, I saw a thin, good-looking man in a pin-striped suit striding toward me. He was already half-way across the road before I realized it was Ted. My, my, I thought, he's aging nicely (graying temples and all).

"Ted?" I asked. "What are you doing here?"

"I've moved here, didn't you know? It's nice to run into you. You look *wonderful!*" he exclaimed.

Liar! I thought to myself, you were always after me to lose weight.

"How did you recognize me?" I asked, instead of, "It's been a long time."

"Oh," he answered, "you're still wearing the coat you had when we first met."

God, the ultimate reality! It's the coat he spotted, not my beautifully familiar face or body, I thought. What luck to run into him now! We exchanged family information, said we would meet sometime for coffee (knowing neither of us would call the other) and pecked each other good-bye with good wishes.

Running into a flesh-and-blood reminder of my past had stopped me cold. I wondered what he had told his wife about me in the past and what impressions she had formed. Well, there was nothing for her to feel competitive about today!

Another point to consider is this: if you have fallen in love with a man who speaks ill of his ex-mate, chances are that those first impressions will aready have become cemented into your imagination. This negativity is extremely hard to get past, even if the woman is completely pleasant. A positive change of heart will come about only slowly, and for the competitive feelings described earlier, that may even suit you. The point is, within the blended family circle, the pattern of relating is first established by what you say about your ex-spouse. As much as there may be a need for you to feel understood or to voice deeply-felt hurts, it might be wise to carefully consider just to what length you should go.

Despite the fact that ex-wives basically fall into two categories, the hostile and the friendly, that still leaves a lot of room for personalities. Take, for example, my friend Sylvia.

Sylvia has a friendly ex-husband who still comes around to chat with Sylvia and her second husband, Joe. Sylvia also has a girlfriend, Jan, to whom she confides all because they have known each other since childhood. Jan decides to entrust Sylvia with stories about her latest love interest . . . Sylvia's ex! The friendship between the two women is severely tested, and although Sylvia admits she initially reacted with strong mixed feelings, "all's well that ends well," and ultimately, everyone survives the drama with friendships intact. Soon after, Jan splits with Sylvia's ex (of course confiding every detail to Sylvia). Her ex-husband soon finds a new friend. The last time I saw them all was when Sylvia and Joe gave their annual potluck dinner party. *All* of the above-mentioned were present without any bad vibrations in the air. Now that's a "friendly" situation and while I admired it, I couldn't relate to it at all nor do I wish to try.

When the pendulum swings to such openness, no doubt you will find ex-mates who go to extreme lengths to be cooperative. In *Stepfamilies: Making Them Work*, Erna Paris depicts the sort of first wife who sends favorite recipes enjoyed by her ex to the second wife as well as giving "number two" several hints on how to please him. Although it is true that an ex-wife to some degree always remains either physically or mentally in the background, I consider this an excessive demonstration of goodwill and not "my style."

In dealing with Heather's goodwill, I was known to frequently make the joke that I would have much preferred a nice "healthy hate," at least some good old-fashioned jealousy. After all, isn't that how it used to be before the liberated '80s? Why then did I still encounter baffled looks and responses when contemporaries heard about my amiable relationship with Heather? (Apparently Heather received similiar reactions from her co-workers.)

Heather's generous attitude did reach its limit (mine, that is) when, after the birth of our first child, she called me from work, wondering how the delivery had fared. "How did it go?" she asked. "David didn't say much of anything!" I was astonished at her genuine involvement with my life and felt uncomfortable as I described my transition into motherhood. Several days later, I was awed when I received many of Robert's most beautiful baby clothes, ones she had been saving in her cedar chest. What was I to do? Send them back when we both knew how badly I needed them? It was a remarkable gesture, but I asked myself if I would have been able to give up my child's clothes to a former husband's new wife.

The truth was I had but one reality to face: David had been married to a truly nice person. Just because they were no longer together didn't mean that she stopped being nice. For that matter, Linda had also been a nice person (her reserve simply being her nature); and perhaps, I wasn't in my heart of hearts as nice as I would have liked to have believed. Otherwise, why the discomfort?

It is only since I myself have become a mother that I have given any real consideration to a "mother's viewpoint" in all of this. It was also for her children's welfare that Heather made such an effort to keep the atmosphere relaxed. Elizabeth and Robert were able to talk freely, show Daddy their rooms and things. All of this reinforced the belief that they had two homes in which they could come and go without reservation. I had to wonder, too, if Heather had internalized any guilt about denying her children a normal family life and, for this reason especially, wished to compensate by making the arrangements as pleasant as possible. I know that David felt badly.

Family Gatherings

It goes without saying that if a friendly ex remains forever in the shadows of your second marriage, then to a larger or lesser degree, so do some of your new spouse's ex-relatives, friends or associations he shared before you met. For you, that may mean shadows, hostile or friendly. Even if you don't actually meet these people, you'll hear about them anyway in conversation with the children. In my case, I had a memorable meeting with most of Heather's immediate family one Christmas, early in my marriage.

In order to see Elizabeth and Robert on Christmas, David and I arranged to spend some time with them in Heather's home. We planned to stay the afternoon and make our way back home early in the evening. Heather was expecting her family for a Christmas buffet after we were due to leave. As the hour drew near, Heather urged us to stay for dinner, reassuring me that they would love to meet me. David hadn't seen his former in-laws for a long time and seemed receptive; Elizabeth and Robert were thrilled with the idea, so we accepted.

In theory, I thought it would be just fine, and on a surface level it was. I found myself chatting with mother, father, brother and auntie, whose eyes would intermittently be fixed on me when they thought I wasn't aware of it. (No doubt, I was more than a little paranoid about being

assessed.) Immediately, I realized that these were wonderful people — but I was the odd woman out. Naturally, they
were eager to hear from David about his family: "How
were Aunts Vera, Lorna and Irma? What had happened to
Uncle Fred, and David's brother Ralph?" Suddenly, I felt
myself acutely distanced from the bunch of them, including
David, and wished instead that I was sitting and listening
to my parents talking about people meaningful to me. The
worst of it was that I blamed myself for being childish
enough to resent the family scene — or was it more that
I resented David for feeling so comfortable? He was supposed to be "my man," an ally there. As it was, he didn't
appear to be concerned about me (or my feelings) in the
slightest. I was in a "snit" all the way home.

What was I trying to live up to anyway? There was a
lesson for me in that evening. Playing "super-tolerant,
'80s-style second wife" clearly didn't sit as well with me as
I had imagined. My competitive nature had surfaced again;
I was trying to match Heather in her ability to be open. I
felt resentful toward her for handling the combined families better than I. Also, I was angry with myself for not
being able to live up to what I thought were the "shoulds"
of my situation: I *should* try to be gracious always. I *should*
show everyone I can rise to the occasion. We *should* all be
one happy family! On that evening at least, all I ended up
feeling was that I *should not* have stayed — it had made me
uncomfortable.

The good that came from it was that I asked myself for
the first time, what kind of relationship did *I* wish to have
with Heather, irrespective of anyone else's needs in the
family? This was a big developmental step for me, because
in my former relationship I had been a sheep on many
occasions. Paul always wanted my companionship in the
car to Linda's (this was Grace Kelly's twin, remember?),
and although the drive and the encounter didn't appeal to
me, I went along to please. Often I found myself patiently
waiting in the car, while he battled out child-care issues
with her on the front porch. As well, I passively went
along with almost every parenting decision he made on

the weekends his son stayed with us, while I did much of the nurturing.

This brings me to a very significant aspect of stepparent/ child relationships: the expectation each has of the other. And how difficult these expectations are to live up to.

In striving to please those people whom we love, we sometimes unwittingly accept roles which really do not allow free expression of our "essence" or "inner self." The expectations which are self-imposed or imposed by others, may continually inhibit us from relating in a real way. Measuring up may be one of the biggest anxieties in a blended family situation. This is true for adults as well as children. From the perspective of my parental window, I have often failed to meet the standards I've set for myself. In those instances where my children or stepchildren had the same standards, the feelings that I had disappointed my family doubled. I used to joke and say I had a "Ph.D. in guilt," even though I believe that the self-beatings we inflict upon ourselves are a waste of creative energy. Learning to redirect this negativity has been difficult for me to do, when my mother, after whom I fashioned my young thoughts, also has the same problem.

Roles, Labels And Breaking The Mold

The child of divorce, who has seen family crumble, must deal with guilt and role-playing too. The two most significant people in life have separated, and it is very disillusioning. After many shed tears, this child may create a tough skin or a role to play which was not needed before. The adult also may react by adopting a tough skin in fear of showing their real self. And so the facade continues, perhaps until the child has played the role so well it truly seems *real* to the adult. My mistaken interpretation of Elizabeth's feelings illustrates this process very well.

As long as I had known her, Elizabeth always "mothered" her brother Robert. This role was one she willingly accepted when both were preschoolers in private home day-care while their mother was at work. Elizabeth had always taken care of Robert, protected him and disciplined him. This in itself gave her an appearance of maturity, far beyond other small children of her age. When Elizabeth and Robert spent weekends with us, she naturally assumed the same responsibilities, ever-watchful over Robert. When Adam and Annie were born, she cheerfully offered to help me watch them. But I noticed too, that she very much enjoyed going shopping with me on occasion leaving the brood behind. Elizabeth also spoke with fondness of her Nan, with whom she drank tea and watched "Coronation Street."

While shopping one day, I introduced Elizabeth to my friend Wanda.

"This is Elizabeth, our eldest, and *such* a big help."

Elizabeth accepted my compliment quietly. Later, I asked my friend for her impression of Elizabeth.

"I don't think she always likes playing the good little girl role," she offered. "I think I almost saw her wince when you gushed about how good she was."

My friend suggested that I try introducing her as just Elizabeth and let others form their opinions.

The discussion with Wanda had given me something to think about. Perhaps, in my eagerness to remark on the qualities I so appreciated about her, I had saddled Elizabeth with the role of being "Little Miss Perfect" in our home. Had I really taken away her freedom to act "wild," "wacky," or "unfeminine"? I chastised myself, recalling my own experiences as the eldest of three daughters. Throughout my high school years I was often obliged to take my sister everywhere. No amount of praise my mother might have lavished upon me in front of her friends would have impressed me. I was the after-school caretaker and didn't enjoy it! Over the years, I had forgotten the feeling. Remember your Ph.D. in guilt, I told myself; you've seen her run and shout with the younger ones on countless occasions. I was too shy to discuss it with her at the time, but have never publicly gushed over her since.

I recall another visit. This time it was Robert who wanted to play with older boys down our street. Adam was too young to join in and Robert thought nothing of leaving him behind. I became very angry. Why had he come for the weekend anyway, if not to be with his younger brother and sister? Biased, because Adam was my child, put out because he was whining (and I had to listen to it), I was most unsympathetic.

As adults we, too, become burdened by the variety of roles we try to live up to. Heather must have felt the stress over the years. As a single mother and career woman, she looked after the physical and emotional welfare of her children 'round-the-clock. Experts now believe that stress is not necessarily a bad thing. Some of us handle dual pressures well, and Heather proved that. It is when an imbalance occurs and too much is demanded of you in one role (such as motherhood) that you will come to feel what Baruch, Barnett and Rivers, the authors of the book *Lifeprints*, refer to as *role strain*.

Whereas it was once thought that it was not a good idea for women to try to fulfill several roles at once (wife, mother, working person), many of us now thrive on this juggling act and are at our creative peak when all three areas are kept going. Maintaining a balance is the key to avoiding role strain. And keep in mind, too, that whether the role is that of biological parent or stepparent, there will always be someone in the wings prepared to comment on how well you are living up to it (by their standards, of course). For this very reason, it is important to create your own standard and come to know which roles you *wish* to fulfill — not feel you *must* or *should* fulfill.

The danger is that in caring too much about what others might think, we may over-analyze ourselves. In his book *One on One*, Theodore Isaac Rubin describes a three-way mental process which occurs while trying to fulfill a role. One part of us simply "is"; a second part watches the job we are doing (for example: Are we living up to our own standards?); the third part observes others reacting to us (Are we living up to their standards?).

Relate this to stepparenting, and you may worry that your husband, his ex-wife, his children, your children,

both sets of grandparents, as well as friends and neighbors, are all observing how you are fulfilling your role.
This is not necessarily so at every moment, but it is human
to overemphasize other people's opinions. At times, you
may look to others to validate the job you are doing, and
may not be entirely happy until you receive their approval.
I find myself going to David for reassurance whenever
I'm in conflict. However, if I have prejudged myself *guilty*,
chances are his reassurances won't eliminate my doubts.

Think about the people you approach when you need to
discuss a problem. Intuitively don't you already know the
opinion of the person you have chosen? Is it possible,
then, that we look for someone who will mirror what we
perceive to be our truth back to us? In other words, one
who echoes what we *want* to hear. In searching for tolerance then, you find someone tolerant to listen to you. For
gossip? You'll have a friend who does that too. It is a nice
feeling to be understood by another, but you cannot always be guaranteed acceptance or applause. The potential
for criticism, so much a part of any blended family, leaves
its family members vulnerable. For this reason, I feel it is
important to stop playing "three-part inner scrutiny" with
your mind. Instead, try to replace it with practices that
encourage inner harmony. Through meditation, you can
begin to discipline yourself, to go within first, before looking elsewhere for answers. I continue to struggle with
learning to increase my resiliency, to maintain my perspective on these "role observers," and most of all give
myself some of the compassion that I try to extend to
others. In the words of playwright James M. Barrie, "We
are all failures — at least the best of us are."

Closely related to this concept of roles and judgments
are the labels we sometimes place on others. As well, we
may unconsciously have a negative reaction to labels that
are placed upon us. "Stepmother"and "stepchildren" are
two with emotionally negative connotations. When first
applied, they make us feel uncomfortable, a little like using
a new married name in our signature.

Years ago, when I was still feeling awkward with the label "stepmother" and in my effort to "blend into" the community, I took great pains to word introductions so as not to use the words: "This is *our* girl, Elizabeth." I allowed strangers to assume that she was my daughter, thereby preventing a third-degree (and it was none of their business, I reasoned).

I thought I was saving embarrassment for Elizabeth as well, and she didn't appear to mind the daughter label. It never occurred to me to ask her how she would like to be introduced or to discuss the issue of labels with her openly. A good discussion sometimes helps to let go of awkward feelings permanently if the stepmother/daughter label makes you uncomfortable.

I did subsequently ask David's children how they referred to us at school. Without hesitation I was told that of course Adam and Annie were their brother and sister. They didn't use stepmother in reference to me; I remained simply Angie, Dad's wife.

At some point, very young children within a blended family must come to an understanding of how their reconstituted family works. When Adam was four or five, he could not grasp that David was Elizabeth's and Robert's father. With no friends in a similar situation, he would repeatedly ask me, "Why do Elizabeth and Robert say *Daddy* to *my* daddy? Don't they have their own daddy?" These questions would surface only after a shared weekend, as he became aware that *all* four children were running to the same Daddy. When David returned the older two to Heather, the little ones were puzzled. Adam had logically decided that if Elizabeth and Robert didn't share the same mother with him, they should also have their own dad.

Before my parents became enlightened by popular talk-show hosts (particularly Phil Donahue's controversial programming), they too had some difficulties with the complexities of our kinship. I understood this, as they are essentially products of an old-world European culture which still views divorce as shameful, and children of divorce as "waifs to be pitied." It has been a gradual process of adjustment for my parents. Ten years ago, they avoided discussing Elizabeth and Robert with their friends. Close friends knew, of course, but as believers in a tight inner family circle, they did not feel comfortable going into lengthy detail with mere acquaintances. It was a mystery to my mother, in the early days, how easily I could "reel out" introductions for my stepchildren: "This is Robert, my husband's son from his former marriage. Robert and his sister live in Toronto with their mother and are with us for the weekend." (Don't you know, Mom, that I mentally rehearsed it before David and I married?)

What has happened to people like my parents is that over the years, they have been watching their children *break the mold*. This term has been coined by authors Susan Gettleman and Janet Markowitz in their book, *The Courage to Divorce*. It means that stepparents, ex-wives and husbands are all beginning to reject traditional attitudes about divorce and thus shed old behavior patterns. Old views would have you think that if a stepmother is kind, then she *must* be trying to replace the biological mother. According to these views, *all* ex-wives are out to kill, or for money. And don't you know that an ex-wife only cooperates if she has ulterior motives? I would like to think that these attitudes were left behind with *Cinderella* and *Snow White*; realistically, they are still with us on some levels.

Grandparents And Former In-Laws

For grandparents, the process of acceptance is painful too. The upheaval of a divorce leaves them with scattered ties. Thanksgiving dinner will never be the same again. From their viewpoint, they have little guarantee when they will see their grandchildren, not to mention who's coming for dinner. They ask themselves whether they should maintain a close relationship with their former daughter/son-in-law, when their adult child is bringing his new love into the house as well. With no set rules or guidelines to follow, it is no surprise that parents of their generation prefer to cling to rigid, more closed attitudes.

My own experience forced me to come to yet another rude awakening about in-law attitudes. I refer here to my past, and now non-existent relationship with Paul's mother. From the moment I was first introduced to her, she welcomed me without reserve. Over the years, I was the recipient of her generosity and friendship, and to whatever degree I could express it, I returned her love. I was enjoying her acceptance of me too much to question the reality that her relationship with Linda had severed abruptly. I was aware though that Paul had asked his parents not to entertain his former wife, viewing it as a sort of betrayal of our relationship. Thus, his mother patiently waited for him to bring her grandson Brendon for visits.

When my relationship with Paul ended, so did my bond with his son Brendon and my friendship with Paul's mother. Whatever else this scenario might say about Paul's power or insecurity, it was now my turn to understand the subtle but clear message: my visits would only create an awkward atmosphere. I would like to fantasize even today that Paul's mother misses me terribly, but I understand where her deep loyalties lie. "Angie," she used to say, "if you want to remain close to our son *always* accept his wife, no matter what you may think of her." There is no question in my mind that she gave Paul's next companion as much warmth as she had given me. She could have been an obstacle for me but wasn't (God knows, I had no difficulty creating my own). And so I thank her for the lesson and hope I will give my children the same kind of support, whether they divorce or not.

Is it really necessary to sever ties with in-laws? My friend Allen, for example, claims that his in-laws dote on him still, more so him than their daughter. In fact, now that he and his wife are divorced, he encourages them to maintain closeness with his ex-wife rather than him. And Heather has managed to maintain a good rapport with David's mother.

As for Paul's mother, losing her helped accelerate the unhooking for Paul and me. Brendon, who was a preschooler when I last saw him, eventually had no memory of our story-times together. Sometimes the love we give leaves little trace, and we must simply learn to "let go and let live."

3

Our Household/Her Household

Man will do many things to get himself loved;
and he will do all things to get himself envied.

Mark Twain

First impressions have been made and comparisons drawn. Both second wife and ex-wife now have some picture (whether distorted or real) of the other's household. Neither is immune to feelings that the "grass is greener," and what children or other family members may say over time, might well plant the seed that one of you seems to be struggling with many more obstacles than the other. Dad, who may feel himself to be in the middle, may even unknowingly through his remarks contribute to the minor resentments which inevitably build up with time.

The Family Pipeline

It is then that this "pipeline," which establishes itself almost from the moment of separation, continues to influence the blended family, both positively and negatively. It seemed to me that at times it took on a life of its own, and that family members and friends were drawn into it.

Both households probably heard more than they should or possibly wished to know.

If this seems distasteful, then one alternative is to instruct the children not to talk about their lives at home or their visits at Dad's place. What parent really wishes to repress their natural chatter? Children, however, sense tension and may hold themselves back if they become aware that their stories are affecting Mother and Dad negatively.

Despite the fact that for many years I was aware of the continual back-and-forth flow, I felt safe in the knowledge that Heather did not pry into our lives. I was also careful not to ask personal questions.

Whereas teenage stepchildren may weigh their words more carefully, Elizabeth and Robert, as three- and four-year-old children, exhibited complete spontaneity. Their mother's cooperative attitude encouraged openness as well. David and I also freely allowed ourselves to talk with Elizabeth and Robert about my family and the plans we were making with them. Elizabeth and Robert enjoyed the close relationship I had with my sisters and called them aunt and uncle when they were younger. They were just as happy as Adam upon the arrival of his new baby cousin Dan.

There was less concern about what Heather might think about us than there is in some blended families. We, in turn, came to know through the children's tales of events going on within Heather's household and family circle. Long before meeting them, I came to know about Elizabeth's and Robert's favorite uncle, their aunt in England and maternal grandparents. As I see it today, we had the best of all possible circumstances.

For the moment, let us not consider blended families which live in hostile circumstances, where children dislike each other and enjoy telling tales and where adults harbor grudges. On a simple level, how does the family pipeline operate?

If you are not directly affected by one, it is much like the experience one has with a young child who has been away from the home with a new activity and is later asked about it. I recall the time my four-year-old Annie went on a preschool trip to the maple sugar bush. Although this example involves my daughter, not a stepchild, it illustrates clearly how a pipeline works in a blended family where younger children have visitations.

Annie came home in a great mood:

Annie: "Can I have a drink?"

Mommy: "How was the maple sugar bush?"

Annie: "Good." (Pause) "Can I paint?"

A Few Hours Later:

Annie: "Mommy, we got to taste the maple syrup that ran out of the trees."

Mommy: "That's great, love."

Annie: "But I didn't like the long ride there. Jenny hit me."

By the following day, in dribs and drabs, I am really piecing together quite a good picture of Annie's trip to the sugar bush, what she liked about it, what she disliked. Memory is triggered each day, and comments seem to come as if "out of the blue." By the third day, there is no question that I know *everything* about that darned sugar bush that ever made an impression on my little girl. Quite naturally, she needed to share it just as I needed to hear it. So it is with the pipeline in blended families.

First And Second Wives: Is The Grass Greener?

In my case, this very thing has caused me to feel little jealousies, and though she was unaware of it, I did feel for a time that in Heather's household the grass *was* greener. This was particularly true during the months I was bogged down in Adam's and Annie's infant and toddler stages. When David arrived Friday evening with Elizabeth and Robert, my imagination dwelt on images of Heather, languidly painting her toenails in the bubble bath, reading novels with the stereo tuned into classical music. In my single working days, I had always enjoyed music and good books. These days, music only competed with noisy children. As for reading, I barely made it through an article. Inwardly I would think: Heather has just gone from two children to zero! I've just upgraded from two to four!

This woman's summers seemed even more enviable! Her mother, the children's Nan, took them for weeks at a time to the family cottage. I could just imagine all the things Heather would be able to catch up on during those weeks. Her weekdays were her own while weekends could be spent with Elizabeth and Robert at the cottage.

I did not gain a different perspective on this until a number of years later when David left the children and me for the first time to go moose hunting. For a ten-day period, I suddenly had to cope alone with bedtimes, getting my car going, emergency errands, interceding in the squabbling, as well as a hundred other trivial matters. As a temporary single parent, I was exhausted each evening.

That trip gave me a new appreciation of Heather's position as a single parent. She had an awesome task, and the weekends Elizabeth and Robert came to our household were most likely much-needed breaks, allowing her time to refresh and recharge herself.

Disillusionment And The Dirt Cycle

What frustrated me most during this period was that David and I had arrived at the point in our marriage where everything done by the two of us was done separately in shift work. There seemed so little opportunity to do anything together — just Angela and David together. Instead, I found myself bathing Annie, while David occupied the other children; when I shopped with Elizabeth, David stayed home with the boys. Even some of the activities we did together as a family, we did apart! Picture swimming, for example: David swam in the deep end with the older children while I stayed in the shallow end with the little ones. As for Sunday morning sleeping in — that was an almost forgotten memory.

In short, I gradually came to realize that I was living the life of the "very married," with the added burden of blended family responsibilities, and the competitive/cooperative conflict of imagining Heather had it better than I. This phase of my life peaked with the unforgettable interlude when I offered to take Elizabeth and Robert during their March-break holiday from school.

In two week's time, I was due to give birth to Annie, and I felt like a whale. Still trying to live up to my "Superstepmom" image, I reassured Heather that it would not be too much having three children underfoot. Despite the fact that the children played well together, until David came home to take charge, I was exhausted and spent a good part of each day horizontal. The day-to-day activities of that week have long since faded, except my emotional impressions of Princess Diana's wedding which took place midweek. On a rainy morning, I and a million other women were witnesses to a "real-life" fantasy, much like the one we had re-enacted with our dolls in childhood. As I watched and took note of the cathedral, long bridal train, Diana's great haircut (every detail seemed significant), I felt small, insignificant and destined to "mother" everyone.

Where had the fantasy gone in my life? Was this prenatal depression or a deeper disillusionment? When David and I had met, all that had been important to me was to leave the workplace for home and family. I had it . . . all of it! But not as I had imagined. David couldn't understand my weariness, and at the time, I couldn't begin to explain it.

Penny Kome, author of *Somebody Has To Do It*, could have shed some light on my emotions. According to a survey Kome conducted on housework, my feelings were, in part, the natural reaction of many stay-at-home wives.

From the homemakers who responded to Penny Kome's questionnaire, the overwhelming response was that, on the whole, these women did not feel that they accomplished *anything* in a given day. Why? The cause is the ongoing *dirt cycle* these women deal with. To clean an area, only to be faced with cleaning it again a few hours/days later, is not a very gratifying task, and certainly pales in significance if you have had the pleasure of sitting next to a female real estate agent at a Christmas open house. If this woman appears to juggle motherhood and career nicely, you'll feel worse. If she's your husband's ex-wife, who juggles motherhood and career, as well as having no weight problem, and she made the appetizers herself, you'll have grounds for depression! Bearing in mind that what *appears to be*, never is. It is nevertheless understandable that mothers who choose to stay at home sometimes feel apologetic in the presence of their career-oriented sisters.

Having already proven myself in numerous well-paying jobs prior to staying home, I would not have predicted that I, too, would feel my self-esteem depleted from the sheer monotony of the dirt cycle, as well as the isolation I was feeling while tending to the demands of young children. Magnify this, and you can imagine what some women feel if they have never worked. Some question if they could ever become successful in the workplace. Just like Kome's respondents I, too, felt trapped in a never-ending dirt cycle.

Husbands and preschoolers don't often lavish praise upon us for the fine job we're doing in supplying them with a steady supply of clean underwear. I was now confused by my dissatisfaction. So was David.

I had changed my tune from: "Let's get married . . . I'll stay home, make babies, chili sauce and manpleasing dinners," to "I'm tired . . . housework is boring . . . I want to do something exciting for a change!" As Kome points out, David's baffled response to my unrest is typical of many a husband who is either insensitive or oblivious to the new signals a wife gives out as she comes to a point of transition with her role and feelings about herself. David still assumed our marriage was problem-free at the same time as I was indulging in my "moving-truck fantasy," the one where an imaginary truck parks in the driveway, and two men carry away the things I need (item by item) for a life of freedom, exciting career and travel. By the time I have mused over my new life as cosmopolitan woman of the year, I've already missed my family and come back to reality feeling better.

Jessie Bernard, a well-known marriage researcher, writes that study after study has shown that husbands usually see their marriages in a better light than their wives. This is based on the fact that marriage, for the woman, brings with it a complete change of work, especially if she chooses to leave her career and stay at home. Even if a woman works, society expects her to do most of the domestic tasks. You know the saying, "A working mother comes home from one job to her second job." This juggling act is often expected by her family and is similarly unrewarded in praise. She has the compensation that at least in the workplace she may receive verbal appreciation. If she doesn't, it might be time to analyze why and what can be done about it.

Having just drawn a comparison between the working mother (Heather) and the full-time homemaker (me), who sees herself buried in dirt and at everyone's disposal, I am well aware there are those of you who might disagree with me intensely (and justifiably so). My neighbor Betty, for example, has been a full-time homemaker, quite happily, for 20 years. Over the years, I have envied her ability to look consistently content (although that's no proof). I have observed Betty driving, shopping, raking, baking — while Sam is working, golfing, fixing or coaching. Three boys (four if you include Sam), three lunches, three homework schedules and numerous extra-curricular activities keep Betty too busy to volunteer. I think to myself, she certainly travels more than I do, accompanying her husband on his business trips. That's exactly what I wanted a few years ago. Despite my own restlessness, I genuinely believe that Betty and other homemakers like her can be happy. The noble and blessed profession of full-time domestic engineer is not to be mocked — it is just not for me, I conclude, sometimes sadly.

Luckily for Betty (and Sam and the boys), she is happy. What about the Angelas who have tried to be, but aren't? If we do feel our task is often ungratifying, television commercials try to make us think otherwise: persons getting dressed in a "TV-land family" notice the feel and smell of their garments! Perhaps the writers and promoters of these products recognize the fact that wives rarely receive this kind of response and thus feed on our wish to be acknowledged daily for our hard work. As this hard work is not rewarded with six-month performance appraisals or salary increases, this surely becomes one of the "psychological price tags" we pay for staying at home.

The Delicate Issue Of Money

Another price tag for some wives is the lack of personal, self-generated money. She does not have the same feeling of independence as the working wife who has earned her own salary.

I noticed this most recently at a shop-at-home house party. Next to me sat a young mother who expressed the wish for numerous items, but ordered only the baby-drink tumblers. I knew that she was happily married to a man who gave her ample freedom with his earnings. Perhaps she was on a strict budget, I reasoned. "I don't feel so guilty spending money if it's for the baby," she said confidingly. "It would be different if I were working." Not having earned it herself, this mother would hereafter weigh the necessity of her purchases. Gone is the spontaneous spending of her working days, the sense of freedom she once had with her own money.

Another stay-at-home friend is on a strict allowance system. Tina rebels now and again by using her charge cards, only to answer for her purchases at month's end. Her husband rants and raves like Fred in *The Flintstones*. They both have allowed her to become a Wilma, who always manages to extract money from Fred.

As I am the family accountant in our household, David does not even wish to know where we stand (as long as it's in the black). I am fortunate that my dependency on David's money has not become an issue and that values related to money have not come between us.

Within the blended family and the relationship you have with your children, stepchildren, spouse or ex, money can become a tool which can either alienate or endear. On a deeper level, money is often linked to and becomes symbolic of more important feelings of the mistrust or trust we have toward our spouses or ex-spouses. For a second wife, the potential danger is that her husband's money matters are so intertwined with his past, she may feel powerless. In *Second Wife, Second Best*, respondents to Glynnis Walker's survey wrote letters describing feelings of resentment because their paychecks were contributing toward the comforts of women they cared nothing about.

Money is a difficult issue, especially when a second wife desires to be the other half of a 50/50 partnership, both emotionally as well as financially. The wife needs to feel that with money (as in other household matters), she has his trust to practice good judgment.

The reality is that money does affect every blended family. The poorest people in North America are single mothers and their children. A father's salary can rarely support two families and society has found no simple answers to the problems of supporting the children of broken marriages. David and I have been fortunate that Heather has always shown extraordinary independence and has never used money to manipulate David's right of access to his children. In fact her working made my dream of becoming a stay-at-home mother possible.

Children who are placed in the middle of the destructive sort of manipulation that takes place in many blended families come to view money as a way to exert power over others. We grow by example after all. This is not to say that no one is immune to noticing money or the lack of it, what it can and cannot do for us in our lives. All children become aware of this in any family.

Though I have had little to complain about, money did on occasion become an issue. It would be silly not to acknowledge that over the years, whenever David and I felt the effects of a financially low period, I became more aware that his obligations to Elizabeth and Robert must be honored despite our other monthly expenses. These feelings had nothing to do with how I felt toward the children; they deserved whatever we contributed. Although I had unrealistic expectations of motherhood and marriage, the reality was that our first home was a handyman's special which we fixed up night after night with Adam in tow. It was in these tight periods that I would allow myself to dwell on the fact that we never ate out, never went to cinemas or took trips — things which Heather appeared to be able to enjoy at the time.

If feelings of contentment are sometimes directly related to how secure we feel financially, it follows that in the blended family, the more comfortable we are, the less likely we are to feel envy. Even without money, if the whole of our lives satisfy us, envious feelings are not likely to surface. This brings to mind my own twinges of envy when we returned Elizabeth and Robert to Heather after a two-week cottage holiday. In our absence, she had redecorated Elizabeth's room beautifully. The rest of her home showed order and good taste as well. As we were at a low point, both emotionally and financially just then, I found myself envious.

Circumstances changed and a number of years later, Heather had the opportunity to see our home. We had just completed a kitchen renovation. Our home was situated on a suburban street, well-treed and breezy. Heather remarked on the flower garden and how she missed having one. Indeed her condo was part of another lifestyle entirely. When she left, I sensed that my grass had seemed just a little bit greener to Heather that day.

Unspoken Agreements

Frustration over money can be one of the more sensitive issues for a second wife. If she chooses to stay in the home, she may well come to feel powerless over her lack of personal funds. As a working woman, she may have agreed to remain employed after marriage, so that her husband can manage to support their new lifestyle, which may include owing payments to his children and/or ex-wife. And what of the second wife who began with the initial understanding that she would work, but who becomes dissatisfied further along in the marriage? By upsetting the apple cart, she is reneging on one of the terms of her *unspoken agreement* which is exactly what I did when I became frustrated with my domestic role.

These unspoken mutual agreements within a relationship go much deeper than money. They can be as simple as "You need to work, so I'll get up nights with the baby," or as serious as "For the security you provide me, I will close my eyes to your philandering." For a second wife, it may mean "I will not insist on having children, as you already have three to support," or "I will not object to your monthly dinner meetings with your ex to discuss the children." What appears to be easy to tolerate during courtship may be much more difficult to live out in the long run.

Weekend Chaos: Being On Call

As a weekend stepmother with two children of my own, I came to feel that confusion had struck our household when Elizabeth and Robert arrived Friday evening. By Monday mornings, I was invariably down in the dumps with the disorder and the overload of laundry. It also took Adam and Annie a full day to settle back into their routines.

For me, the most frustrating part of my weekends with David and four children was the pressure of being "on call" most of the time. This was similarly voiced by the mothers who responded to Penny Kome's survey on housework. It was strongly expressed that these women "marked time" while waiting to be "taxi, cook, teacher, peacemaker, etc."; in other words, generally making certain that everyone was doing what they needed to do, getting from here to there. Short periods in between seemed to be mere pockets of time in which I could do little for myself. Clearly, you don't need to be a second wife in a blended family to feel this way about motherhood and housework. On weekends, at least, many women feel stressed by a host of responsibilities and interruptions, and just when they most need a cup of tea!

Despite the chaos, I felt great satisfaction in sharing with David, time spent with *all* of his children. It also gave me joy to witness their playtime together as stepsiblings. In *Sombebody Has To Do It*, Penny Kome reported that one third of her respondents also got similar pleasure from seeing their husbands happy.

It is no secret that unstructured time has always been a problem for me particularly on weekends. I have difficulty imposing routine and discipline. Thus I experienced even more chaos and less time to call my own during our visits with David's children. Stay-at-home stepmothers with good organizational skills might have had an easier time of it. As it was, I vacillated between feeling happy about having us all together and feeling burdened by extra chores.

It has since occurred to me that Heather, like any other mother not given the choice of working, would not be able to relate to any part of my life at home. Would she have thought my lifestyle was greener than hers? After all, rain or shine, Heather had to appear at the office each day. No doubt she imagined that I had plenty of time for my nails, Monday to Friday, before Elizabeth's and Robert's arrival. Then again Heather didn't have to enroll in a pottery class to reassure herself that new skills could be mastered (outside of learning how to reason with a toddler). It was through working with clay that I regained some of my separate self, unconnected to home and family. The importance of this is not to be overemphasized. Penny Kome's findings showed that those homemakers with the highest sense of well being incorporated rewarding interests and hobbies into their day-to-day lives.

Cooperative Attitudes

As much as happiness in a blended family must be generated from within each individual, the cooperative attitude of an ex-wife also plays a significant role. A self-supporting, independent first wife can do much to make life easier for her former husband. I count my blessings to this day that Heather is one of them. I would have been far less happy had Heather adopted the attitude of my acquaintance, Laura.

Laura stemmed from a generation of females who believed it was necessary, as well as feminine, to completely lean on a man, both financially and emotionally. As a wife she would never have dreamt of working. Instead she busied herself with tennis at the club, gourmet cooking classes and other activities enjoyed by the "almost rich and famous." After fifteen years of marriage, Laura separated from her husband. She claimed at the time that she would do everything within her power to continue "in the lifestyle to which she had become accustomed." During her years of marriage, Laura had remained dependent upon her husband, and as an ex-wife she did also. It was not until she found a new man to whom she could transfer her needs that she was prepared to loosen her hold on her ex-husband.

Another factor crucial to happiness within the blended family is a second wife's attitude toward her husband's children. The influence she has on her husband gives her a subtle power she may, or may not, choose to use. In their book *Surviving the Breakup*, authors Judith Wallerstein and Joan Kelly maintain that a second wife often sets the tone in her household, especially in regard to visitations with her stepchildren. Her cooperative attitude may have much to do in maintaining a father's bond with his children. On the other hand, she may also be the cause of conflicting feelings for him, in which he finds himself torn between his new wife and children. The authors present further evidence that a father's bond with his children by a former spouse becomes more difficult to maintain when young children are present in his new household, particularly with the arrival of a new baby. Over and above anything else, it is in this circumstance that the attitude taken by the second wife is the determining factor.

The compassionate attitudes of stepmothers have been observed by Wallerstein and Kelly, and although I would like to *think* I consistently demonstrated compassion, I didn't always. Certainly, David and I had some common

beliefs for our blended family; we felt it was important to
develop a bond between *his* children and *our* children, and
we tried to convey to Elizabeth and Robert that Adam's
and Annie's births in no way replaced them.

As a new mother, I was naturally preoccupied with the
baby. The truth was that I did not physically have the
same time for David's children as I once had. Nevertheless
I tried not to neglect their feelings. I also had no wish for
David to dote on the baby at the expense of Elizabeth and
Robert. In retrospect our family bond during this phase
became strengthened. Our weekend ensemble came to be
even more of a blended family and, at least in their younger years, Elizabeth and Robert enjoyed the fact that they
were idolized by their younger siblings from the first moment they could articulate their names.

Having established friendly vibrations within our household, David and I juggled mattresses about on floors to
accommodate Elizabeth and Robert each time they came.

Peter Rowlands makes the point in *A Book for Separated
Families* that what adults consider a gross inconvenience is
often seen as an "adventure" by the children. In our household, it was "pajama party" with cramped sleeping bag
arrangements for years. Before Annie was born, we were
even able to fit three little ones into the same bathtub!
Other advice books for blended families recommend that
visiting children have their own "space" or "cubby" to
establish a sense of home away from home.

I personally feel our inability to give Elizabeth and Robert their own rooms made little difference to their feelings
of belonging. I qualify this by adding that their young ages
made them extremely flexible to our lifestyle.

For this reason, I consider myself fortunate. Unfriendly
stepteens create completely different vibrations in a household. Years later, Elizabeth and Robert came to have other
needs, to require other kinds of attention. I found myself
suddenly dealing with strange new children who no longer
mixed as easily with the younger two. New feelings
emerged from all quarters just when I thought I really
had established a neat little status quo in our family.

PART ❧ II:

Reality Sets In

The Itch

After seven years of wedded bliss
My friend Louise has got "the Itch"
And dreams of giving up her home
To make it
On her very own

A classic case, at the best
Of utter marital unrest

"Her husband's boring
She is too
They seldom ever
Coo-chi-coo"
Their lifestyle leaves them little time
For long discussions over wine

With that, Louise broke into tears
Moaning she'd wasted her best years

Then asked me how I had survived
Thirteen long years of married life

I told Louise we lacked the time
I'd need at least one litre wine
"The grass isn't greener" and
"Don't lose your head"
Are the cliches I quoted to my friend instead

Renewed again
She rushed away
With promises for lunch one day
While leaving me
Somewhat depressed
In my own marital unrest
I wish I'd had the heart to say
What she'd find out herself one day
If she could make it through this one
There was another "Itch"
To come!

Angela Neumann Clubb

MAPLE RIDGE
FAMILY EDUCATION CENTRE
22342 SELKIRK AVENUE
MAPLE RIDGE, B.C. V2X 2X8

▶ **4**

Personal Freedom/Family Ties

Life is a tragedy for those who feel,
and a comedy for those who think.

Jean de la Bruyere

During this period of our lives, when I was asked how many children I had, I frequently responded humorously with "two part-time, two full-time." I immediately followed this with a brief explanation of how our blended family worked. Typical responses were: "What an interesting household you must have . . . However do you all manage to get along? . . . Doesn't it bother you to associate with your husband's ex-wife? . . . Do the children fight?"

To the world at large, I gave the impression that we had our act together; and yes I could admit with some pride, we did all get along. Heather gave me no nightmares and the children obviously cared about one another.

However, I could not put my finger on why I was beginning to experience a growing sense of disillusionment. Was a holiday as good as a rest? Taking all four kids to my folks' cottage, as we had done in previous summers, was not the answer. In retrospect these holidays only exaggerated the symptoms of my weariness.

55

Over the years my parents had always generously offered to share their cottage with the family, observing
their rules of course. My mother is by far a fussier house-
keeper than I, and it was important for me to take care of
the cottage as she would. Picture then, a chalet-style summer home with wall-to-wall carpet, large picture windows
and nicely furnished bedrooms (complete with individual
thermostat controls). With four children in tow, all under
the age of seven, how could I possibly maintain my parents' standards and still enjoy myself? Daily trips to the
beach, mounds of laundry and playthings all over added to
my accumulating fatigue.

My parents would frequently join us for the weekend,
along with my two sisters. Having let the place "go" from
Monday to Thursday, an acute case of "cleaning anxiety"
which struck each Friday morning, had me behaving like
an unhappy shrew, scurrying around trying to get the
cottage up to par (and never managing). This pattern
repeated itself every weekend. I never did allow myself
to completely relax, and being a glutton for punishment,
I added to my workload full-course barbecue dinners each
evening. I now wonder what on earth I was trying to live
up to in those days. Wieners on a stick would have been
just fine!

And where was it written that we always had to include
Elizabeth and Robert in my only two-week holiday with
David? It was another status quo we had set up for ourselves in order that we might really become the ideal
blended family. It was difficult to break this tradition years
later. Once again, David appeared more satisfied than I
because the mere change in scenery and the cottage lifestyle gave him a much-needed break from his work envi-
ronment. He could do little about the fact that I felt I had
simply transferred my chores from one location to another.

Our beginnings as a couple, and those early day trips to
the zoo with Elizabeth and Robert, had become history. In
our efforts to amass possessions and establish our place
in the community, life had become far too serious. I used
to play a game with my stepchildren, one which my

former stepson Brendon had shared with his father. Before picking up Elizabeth and Robert, I would hide loose Smarties in my pocket. "What's in your ear?" I would ask one of them. As if by magic, I managed to extract a Smartie. "Me next!" the other would urge. "Is there a Smartie in my ear, too?" How I accomplished this trick was a mystery to them for years. Now, several years later, Adam and Annie had never experienced the Smartie game. I had missed the boat.

Had I forgotten how to play? Unlearned how to live more in the moment as I had once been able to do? As I reflected on this, I realized that I had been oblivious to the transition which had caused a shift in my thinking: what I had formerly considered as "play" had been re-categorized as "work." In the early days with Elizabeth and Robert, I had both "played house" and "played stepmother." Later, I had to work at it and spontaneity had fallen by the wayside.

Mother Love And Stepmother Love

Another truth I had to acknowledge to myself was that my tolerance level was higher and better for my natural children. Petty grievances which I might have overlooked in Adam and Annie, irritated me with Elizabeth and Robert. And as much as I was aware of this, I was terrified that it would show and went to great pains to try to appear fair and equal. The fact was, however, that repressing my irritation only made me look "up-tight" at times, and because I felt I should not express anger or negativity toward my stepchildren, no one in the house knew why I was tense.

As I see it now, what was going on is what psychologists call *denial*. I was not prepared to let my stepchildren or my family see that I simply didn't have the same kind of love or emotional investment in Elizabeth and Robert as I had for my natural children. What I didn't understand was that it was OK to love them differently, even to communicate this difference if the atmosphere was right for such a discussion. On an inner level I had prejudged that admitting my love for Elizabeth and Robert was not the same would mean I was somehow declaring to the world that I loved them far less than my own children. This would not have been true, as others knew and felt that I cared deeply.

As I came to terms with my feelings, I began to acknowledge to myself that my own children could (and do) walk all over me and I would still be deeply committed to their growth. Love came naturally with my own children, and although it was very easy to love Elizabeth and Robert, it was something I decided I would like to do. Emotionally, I worked at my relationship with them. I did not allow myself to yell at them, but certainly let myself go with my own children. I reasoned that I had far more right to demonstrate control or teach my kids. Harnessing myself, as I did with Elizabeth and Robert, also stifled the openness between us, and sadly, also the degree of love I felt at times.

Involvement/Non-Involvement And Your Needs

For whatever reason a second wife initially becomes involved with her husband's children (to please him, to be a good sport, because he expects it, or because she really cares for them), over time she is required to make many adjustments. Her relationship with them will continue to develop, for in my experience there is no such thing as a fixed relationship with one's stepchildren. I have always fluctuated between being able to give them a good deal of my energy and caring, to feeling depleted and having little in reserve left for them.

In his book *How to Succeed As a Stepparent*, author Peter Jolin feels strongly that a stepparent's primary responsibility is to himself; anything he does with the stepchild should essentially be in his own interest as well the child's. The author justifies his remarks by qualifying that he does not condone selfishness on the part of the stepparent.

My own conclusions to his remarks are mixed; I see myself after all as the "all-time family marshmallow." What I do understand as valid and closer to his point is the concern that I as a stepmother might "lose myself" in trying to adapt too much to Elizabeth's and Robert's needs. Mothers and stepmothers need to heed this advice. Mothers who "love too much" ultimately hurt themselves. His cautionary words are appropriate to all mothers.

In the past I have allowed myself to be pulled in two directions: what I wanted to do for me and what my children wished me to do. I understand that I had freedom of choice, but I have also been conditioned since childhood by what my own parents have said and done, to believe that parenting brings with it minor and major sacrifices which *must* be made. When I accepted the role of stepmother, I unconsciously brought along these same values.

Thus I cannot do as *How to Succeed as a Stepparent* would imply; that is, always consider my needs first. I will always be prepared to make some sacrifices for Elizabeth and Robert and consider this simply a part of parenting. In this way, although not every member of my family was able to experience total satisfaction all the time, at least I felt the children understood we were prepared to try. When Elizabeth and Robert came to see us, I like to think they noticed the times David didn't feel like swimming at the pool but chose to freeze nonetheless. Realistically, they will not fully understand how their wishes did matter until they themselves are parents.

In dealing with Elizabeth and Robert, no doubt my genuine feelings, as well as the superficial ones, did not always come across. Perhaps when they are older, they will understand me, I reasoned. But for now, how could the accumulated effects of several years "on call" and my feelings of frustration be something they could relate to? Children are far more resilient than adults at times. When David brought Elizabeth and Robert on Friday evenings, I did not accomplish the mental switch-over as readily as they. My Monday-to-Friday world had its own rhythm, over which I had some control. I relinquished it on these Friday evenings when my household instantly transformed itself — in both noise level and in pace. Secretly I wished that I could leave everyone behind for a few hours to do something alone. My inner "shoulds" dictated I should stay put to direct traffic, unroll sleeping bags and prepare late dinner. As I see it now, I had set myself up to be indispensable, only to resent it when I was.

Eventually, on David's urging, I did visit a girlfriend out of town every now and then. I fretted and felt my share of guilt at first, but later came to realize that David was holding down the fort quite efficiently. Because I had created an atmosphere of tension in the past, when I did visit my friend and returned a happier person, David too had enjoyed being with his children more in my absence. This period of occasionally distancing myself was good for us all. Knowing that I could leave the family for a time when I wished did much to ease my tension. I had reinstated my sense of freedom and choice.

My view is that each stepmother begins her life in the blended family with two choices regarding her stepchildren: to make an effort and thereby participate or to make no effort and disassociate herself from the activities her husband shares with his children. If he insists on her involvement, giving her no choice, she may well react unhappily, if for no other reason than that he has denied her the freedom to choose to give of herself. At best it becomes a begrudged effort on her part.

I cannot imagine a second wife who would initially not desire to be liked and not make an effort. Much of her attitude, too, will be determined by the ages of the children and how they treat her at the onset. If circumstances are favorable and a second wife does not try too hard to impress, the relationship with the children may begin to show signs of compatibility. If she does not enjoy being around the children, it will soon become obvious to all. In that event, it would be far better for everyone if she opted out of visitation times (for a time at least), so that the non-custodial parent can achieve as much closeness as possible with his children under the circumstances. Weekend stepfathers, too, have the same choices.

Non-involvement in the long term, however, will not be totally satisfying. The biological parent may come to feel a sadness that things could not after all have turned out differently, and the second wife will feel herself alienated from an inner circle whose happy times she can only imagine. Making the effort and working at a compassionate outlook toward stepchildren seems to be the better alternative to me.

Guilt

In coming to understand my own emotions, I see now that until I arrived at the point where I could physically propel myself to leave the family for a few hours, a rather destructive cycle had developed.

My self-image dictated that I should become the perfect stepmother. My roles as wife and mother dictated that I must be there for David, our children and the household tasks. David was not demanding this of me — I was. Consequently when I came to feel restless and dutybound, an inner conflict always ensued. While one inner voice expressed the wish to get away from it all, another chastised my selfishness: "That's your role as a mother. What's the matter with you? They are nice children and you should be happy to do it."

The conflict surfaced in tension. I magnified our difficulties by not wishing to admit my feelings to David, who spent much of these weekends trying to double-guess me. Quarrels over trivia came between us, and although I did not wish for it, David bore the brunt of much of my inner frustration and repressed anger. This, in turn, created a mutually destructive cycle in which we both felt guilt: I for letting my negative emotions spill over onto David, he for creating more work for me when his children came to visit. Aside from stifling spontaneity, I came to feel responsible for a family boomerang pattern in which David and I often spoiled a potentially good weekend by feeling guilty.

The destructive aspects of guilt have been observed by numerous professionals. In *Compassion and Self-Hate*, Dr. Theodore Isaac Rubin points to fear, guilt and shame as being the major three forces in life which cripple us. Dr. Willard Gaylin in his book *Feelings*, makes a distinction between shame and guilt, when he points out that shame is a much more private matter, whereas guilt requires us to communicate our feelings before we can dilute it. It was just such a weekend when I did communicate my feelings to Elizabeth and Robert and in doing so, shocked David.

It would be naive to think that, after numerous years of participation in our household, Elizabeth and Robert would not have become aware of tension between David and myself. These tensions sometimes had nothing at all to do with blended family issues. We were reluctant to hash our problems out openly in front of them (and they stayed up too late for us to do it after their bedtime!). Scathing words and significant tense glances were what David and I often resorted to. It wasn't much better that weekend. Elizabeth coped by becoming super quiet. Robert distracted himself with Adam.

One afternoon, I had to comment: "Some of these visits are *the pits* for you, aren't they?" What were they to say? I received no response. Yet this comment in itself did much to alleviate the tense atmosphere and confirmed for me what I had always known: children have much more difficulty in dealing with a vague understanding, wondering if they are at fault, than knowing explicitly where they stand. The few words of reassurance I gave them right then were what they needed to hear; that everything was basically all right, and more importantly, that *they* hadn't caused it. David, although not capable of the same degree of openness, did not object to the few times I opened up and really expressed my feelings.

Anger

Anger, because it is so frequently felt by all of us, deserves to be fully understood. In *Compassion and Self-Hate*,

Rubin writes about this emotion in some detail. According to Rubin, anger not fully vented becomes *repressed anger*, and this is a dangerous thing for any relationship. If anger goes inward, it then takes on other more destructive forms such as recrimination, self-hate, guilt and sabotage. To a degree, at least, this is exactly what had happened to me. Feeling family-bound had created within me feelings of anger toward David and the children. Because I loved my family, I felt it was unacceptable to show my anger, and it festered within. My self-esteem suffered because I blamed myself for feeling angry at all.

Another dangerous consequence of anger happens when a second wife allows the anger felt toward her husband's ex-wife to overflow onto her stepchildren. A second wife who does not deal with an ex-wife directly, but feels resentment toward her just the same, has no healthy way to express this emotion. She could communicate her anger to this woman, but quite possibly won't wish to.

A husband is not exempt from repressing anger. Perhaps he fears showing his anger toward an uncooperative ex-wife. So as not to make matters worse, he represses it and may unwittingly let it out on his new mate, who innocently becomes his whipping post or sounding board. This is exactly the role I played with Paul during his battles with Linda. As he was attempting to disengage himself from her financially, it was I who listened for hours to his grievances against her. I ask myself now, where was *I* when I allowed this to happen? I suppose on some level I was relieved it wasn't me he was angry with. On yet another level, it likely reassured me that he had indeed fallen out of love with his wife who, as the cliche goes, "never fully understood him anyway."

It takes just one person in a blended family venting a stream of repressed anger for others to become affected. I shall never forget the time when Heather surprised us all.

As far as repressing emotions like anger is concerned, her track record had always been better than mine. Not the slightest recriminatory remark had passed her lips in the years I had known her. In all that time, she had been so accommodating to David, even my mother was jealous! Her outburst came over David's time schedule bringing Elizabeth and Robert back to Toronto. We were renovating the kitchen that day and had had floor-laying troubles. David, not realizing she had car repair difficulties, blurted out, "But I *must* bring them home by three o'clock!" That remark was the catalyst:

"Now you listen to me, David . . . You are a . . . and I've just about taken enough of your . . . I should have said this years ago . . . If you think you can . . . you are sadly mistaken . . ." and so it went. It took David only a few hours to recover. It took me much longer.

There is no question that Heather had expressed real feelings she had done a good job of suppressing. My reaction was one of genuine alarm; I saw this as a sign that she could no longer be trusted to be as cooperative as before. I continued to worry about a repeat incident months after the hurricane had come and gone. For the first time in my relationship with David, I felt negatively toward Heather, and her children knew it.

Gossip

I became acutely aware of the pipeline and didn't wish our family's business to be conveyed to Heather. Although I never openly put her down, it was clear that I had become more guarded. Elizabeth and Robert, sensing this, stopped sharing stories about their mother. It was a sad thing to experience and didn't right itself until the day I finally admitted to Elizabeth that her mother had made me very angry too. Like a stone thrown in a pond, Heather's repressed anger had created ripples which affected the atmosphere in our entire blended family. Being able to admit my own negative feelings to Elizabeth allowed me to take the first step in re-establishing some of the good-will which had been lost. I see now that Heather's anger had created a cause-and-effect cycle which resulted in my own repression of anger. I hadn't wanted to gossip. It was one of our family "no-no's," but perhaps a healthy dose of gossip would have repaired family feelings earlier.

Gossip does have a way of becoming addictive, and it can be a destructive expression of anger. We *all*, at times, have been destructive, terribly repressed, angry people. Each of us is guilty of gossip at some point in our lives.

Though I make an effort not to gossip now, I used to enjoy gossiping about Paul after we had separated. We now time-shared a wonderful woman, Tessa, who had been a close friend to us both when we lived together. Poor Tessa had to bite her tongue to keep our stories private. She couldn't always manage it. When I first found out Paul was with a quiet, tiny, sensitive woman who catered to his needs completely, I felt the bond of sisterhood with her immediately. Loving him required a lot of energy, I thought, but don't be so passive! Old wounds and pride compelled me to ask Tessa to relay only the good things about my life, such as my accomplishments (to dispel any smug illusions he might have had about my not being able to do superbly without him). It is easy for me to recognize now that gossiping about Paul was my own way of dealing with unfinished business, feelings which were never expressed to him directly before we separated.

Engaging in gossip is a temptation in most blended families; the pipeline feeds this temptation. Private negative remarks and exaggerations remained private between David and myself. Though I never liked myself for this, it was a way of taking the lid off some of the pressure and anger that had accumulated. I am sure that most of us are truly nice people; we do not wish to gossip maliciously, but doing so provides an outlet for our emotions once in a while. Why do we do it? We are inclined to gossip about someone who has hurt our feelings in the past. Sometimes morals and values ingrained in childhood keep us from openly expressing our feelings toward that person, feelings that surface in the form of gossip.

An example of this in my life is a basic family law I was taught to observe all through childhood: *never argue with or insult your elders*. If, then, an older member of my family hurt me, because I was conditioned as a child to respect my elders, I had a hard time expressing my anger toward that person. Similarly, if I became involved in a discussion with an elder, my childhood conditioning dictated that *before* the discussion became an argument, I, as the younger person, *must* acquiesce (whether he or she was right or not). If this person had attacked my views, for example, gossip not only alleviated the injustice of my not being able to "talk back" but also my repressed anger.

Another example of this kind of gossip is when a wife, who has been offended by her mother-in-law and who has failed to assert herself, later does a "post-mortem" of the conversation with her husband as the sympathetic listener. Her need for support and reassurance is easy to understand and God help him if he doesn't give it!

Of the many ways anger can be expressed, there is yet another, more devious way of venting it; we can mask our anger with honesty. "Back-door honesty" in a blended family occurs when one parent tells his child unpleasant "truths" about the other, while at the same time rationalizing that the telling of it is ultimately for the *good* of the child. This is a self-deceptive and blatantly destructive form of anger. It can only harm the child, who now has to cope with the love he feels for the discredited parent and the awful "truth" he must now accept about that adult. We are all familiar with someone in our lives who has told us a painful truth in the name of love.

If an obese woman's husband repeatedly reminds her of her size in order to be "helpful," one would also have to question his feelings. As most weight watchers will confirm, they are already too aware of this truth.

Negative Feelings And Sexuality

One more important and possibly unexpected area where anger expresses itself between two adults is sexuality. Authors Grace Baruch, Rosalind Barnett and Caryl Rivers, in their book *Lifeprints*, have found that one of the first signs of repressed anger is sexual dysfunction. For a woman, this anger may manifest itself in lack of sexual interest, inability to achieve orgasm or in frigidity. For a man, it shows itself in premature ejaculation or impotency. In either case, whether it poisons a couple's sex life or not, feelings of anger would seem to indicate that there is a crucial need to talk — openly and honestly. Put aside for a moment alarming words like "impotency" and "frigidity" and it becomes easier to deal with the reality that our physical demonstrations of love are one of the first areas affected when we are angry or hurt.

How can a woman who feels housebound on weekends through trying to catch up with chores or who exhausts herself with a full day's work at the office, only to come home to maneuver her kids from Brownies to bathtub, feel romantic? Inwardly, she may feel angry that she has no time for herself. How romantic does a second wife feel who juggles the same schedule and who is also expected to be supportive to her husband when he brings his children for a weekend? A weekend away in the Honeymoon Suite with the heart-shaped jacuzzi may be just the right prescription.

I often think about something my mother told me years before I had to worry about such things. Mom owned a gift/toy/hobby store on the main street in the small middle- to upper-class town where we lived. After twenty-five years of my mother's business, most kids had received birthday presents from her store, and she had been able to observe them and their parents growing up. Young stay-at-home mothers brought their toddlers in and, in between the hundred "Don't touch" commands, tried to get their shopping done. They seemed so frazzled at times; these moms could barely exchange short chats with another mother.

"You know, Angela, it's an interesting thing to see," my mother told me. "A mother with young children comes for years, looking rushed, tired and just not relaxed. A few years later, I'll see the same woman, with a good manicure, a white pant suit, looking younger and better than I ever saw her when she had babies."

With exceptions of course, my mother became aware of the fact that mothers with young children don't always pamper themselves as they did when childless. Once the children become older, they begin to take more interest in their bodies, in fashion, and can even dare to wear white again. On this point, a working mother has a decided advantage; she is more motivated to look her best.

We all attempt to shake the "mold" and re-do our image at various times in our lives, some of us to a larger or lesser degree. I broke it the time I dyed my hair orange. It happened one unfortunate afternoon, during the period when I was very unhappy with my relationship with Paul. I felt powerless to make things better, but yearned for some tangible change. It would be nice to have hair like Samantha Eggar, I thought. But, my hairdresser hadn't seen the movie *The Collector*. Samantha had been captured by a lunatic butterfly collector who wanted to possess her so much that he locked her in the basement along with his collection until her creative spirit died. (There's a Freudian slip in this story, I think.) I still wanted Samantha's hair color: "Can you picture a beautiful Irish Setter?" I asked my hairdresser. "Yes, of course. We'll make you look like an Irish Setter," she reassured me. Two hours later, I looked like an orange lantern — I really had broken the mold this time.

When I had my moments with David, I knew well enough to leave my hair alone. I had learned to take some freedom for myself on my weekends away to visit my good friend out of town, and I also had a potter's wheel which for many months gave me a lot of personal pleasure. But there was something missing still, and it would come to me as soon as I understood what I was looking for. After five years together, our blended family had reached a new plateau; everyone was content with the status quo except me. I determined to instigate a change and found it after a family holiday in Coboconk, Ontario.

5

Work And Motherhood

Strange how little a while a person can be contented.

Mark Twain

For the first time in our family history, David and I rented a cottage, sight unseen, at a resort in the Kawartha area. At the time, my parents felt a little wounded: "What is it, you don't like it with us anymore? We didn't get uptight with the sand inside the cottage — *you* did . . . So much money you're spending, and then you tell us you need to save? . . . Well, if you really must be that private, what can we say? Is it because David doesn't like the fishing up here?"

Aren't you listening? I thought. It's more than that — it's me! Discovering new territory was just what I told myself I needed. I even thought I might be able to relax at the resort; the brochure had advertised a very nice sauna. David was equally pleased. The Kawarthas have good fishing.

In the car we crammed everything from two week's supply of fresh produce, to playpen and rainy-day games. Mother, Father, Elizabeth, Robert, Adam, three-month-old Baby Annie and our black standard poodle. Waving good-bye to Heather, who had just been to the library for her supply of "good summer reads," didn't even bother me too, too much. We arrived at Coboconk, Ontario, three hours later.

Comparing cottage number seven to my parents' cottage would be similar to likening mackerel to smoked salmon. The walls were uninsulated and paper thin; we froze at night and were forced to stay out all day from the heat inside. Kitchen facilities were inadequate and the shallow swimming area had sand-holes to terrify the little ones. As for the sauna, guests were asked to give one-half hour notice if they wished to use it — at $1.00 per person.

Minor things I was able to take in my stride. The thinness of the walls was responsible for Annie's awakening too early each time Robert watched cartoons at 7:00 a.m. There was also the fact that this "resort" was a mere little strip of property directly off the highway; one could only walk back and forth the length of twelve cottages. It is really disconcerting when various families, all eating their corn on the cob, chew and stare at you walking by (no less than ten times), with your baby in a collapsible stroller. Annie couldn't fall asleep easily in the cottage, particularly as it was as hot as an oven by mid-day. I spent hours walking about endlessly, going nowhere, trying to get Annie to sleep.

David, on the other hand, was going everywhere it seemed; each time he fished he tried a new spot. This is strange, I thought. I had never considered him a selfish person before (but then I had never been around him in consistently fishable waters!) Three times each day, he ventured out. Sometimes he went alone in the evenings, but he usuallly took along at least one child. That still left me with the rest to supervise. This was not the David I had married. How could a man be so oblivious to everything (I meant me) but fishing? At first I tried to feel happy for him. After all, he worked so hard all year, he deserved this time, I told myself.

After a few days I was getting heartburn and became very angry (that's repression and the cooperation/competition conflict, remember?) After five years of marriage,

Mr. Hyde, who had steadfastly stood by my side with home-and-child-care on holidays, was now pullling a *Jeckyll* on me — and "Gone Fishing" was the message. By 9:30 each evening he was contentedly cleaning his catch for next morning's fish-fry. Because of the good, clean, northern air, by 10:00 p.m. he was asleep with the children. With no other recreational facilities to speak of, no mother and no sisters nearby for diversion and my needlepoint finished, I was bored beyond imagination!

Reassessing: What About Me?

When I scanned the rack of used paperbacks for something to read, a romance novel was out of the question. Instead, a subtitle *Predictable Crises in Adult Life* caught my eye. The book was called *Passages,* and it was written by Gail Sheehy. It was unfamiliar to me, but I wondered if this was what I was going through. Midlife crisis? For the remainder of the holiday, I read several chapters each evening after dark. The heat and David's fishing seemed to matter less as I immersed myself in Sheehy's concepts.

My first mistake, of course, was to actually believe I might relieve my pressures by changing cottages. My discontent was a little more complex. Only four years earlier, I had assured David that *all* I desired from life was to become a mother, take care of our home, bake, preserve and decorate. These days the tune I was singing was that when Annie was happily settled into grade school, I might think of working part-time. But that was still six years away. I was thrilled by Annie's birth, yet what was I to do until she entered grade school?

Having arrived at this confusing point, I was now more than willing to open myself up to new answers. It would be an understatement to say Sheehy's book affected me. Not having heard about *Passages* from my friends, I was able to read it with an unbiased mind. As I read, Sheehy led me through the "passages" I had left behind. I came to accept the crucial question I was certainly asking now:

What about me? And quite apart from my family, what did I want to do now?

Throughout my lonely holiday, Ms. Sheehy and I participated in an inner dialogue. I had been confused by my desire to re-enter the workforce, in view of the fact that just four years prior I had wanted out of the career-race so badly. In terms that I could fully grasp, Gail Sheehy helped me understand that I was coming to a new *life passage*. More importantly I also realized that I was not allowing myself to "get on with it." Instead, I was clinging to the old passage: a six-year plan I had made for myself geared to my children and their schooling. My own intuitive voice, however, was urging me to branch out and explore new dreams. Why wait? Sheehy wrote, do it *now!* After much soul-searching, I decided that I did very much wish to keep my flexible schedule by staying home, but I was also going to take steps to find some kind of satisfying new work.

The night before we left Coboconk, I broke David's happy bubble by explaining to him, quite seriously, the conclusions I had come to. As far as I was concerned, if he must overdose on fishing, let him do it with a buddy. From now on, I wanted more emphasis on our relationship during our holidays. Our blended family would have to adjust. I also announced my hopes for finding some kind of work that pleased me. "Perhaps," I told him, "it might be writing."

The most difficult stand I had to take, however, was when I asked David to consider excluding Elizabeth and Robert from the two week holiday trips to cottage country. At first it was a mystery to him why I would want such a change and he objected. It seemed to him that four children were no more work than two. I saw it differently. This was one of the few times I admit to placing my needs first, despite David's initial resistance, and Adam's and Annie's loud objections.

In the interest of creating a close bond among the six of us, we had always vacationed together. Because the older children wanted to stay up and watch television, it left little privacy for David and me. I now felt the time had come to consider our needs as a couple too. Had we had the financial resources, possibly David and I would have recharged our batteries long ago with short weekend trips away to a hotel or inn. Had we wanted privacy badly enough, we might have found a way without a large outlay of cash. Whether this need had developed gradually or surfaced quite suddenly, now appeared to be the time to examine it.

My personal "passage" had compelled me to ask "What about me?" David quietly went about his business. At least he appeared to be calm. (He now admits he really was wondering what I'd end up tackling.) Meanwhile, I was beginning to find some of my answers.

New Passages: Outgrowing Old Beliefs

The first decision was to have David arrange a moose-hunting trip which would allow him unpressured time away, to do what he loved most, be alone in the solitary outdoors.

The second decision was that I felt I wanted to write. But what? My first attempt was an article — so poorly written I didn't have the courage to submit it. For several days I continued to agonize over what to write about until one afternoon I spotted a newspaper piece on the status of Canadian writing. Writers were having a difficult time making a living at their craft it seemed. Amidst the negativism, one sentence literally jumped out at me: "Next to the Bible, the cookbook is still selling." My intutitve voice reacted. This was just the direction I needed. I could write a cookbook! Before I had the chance to break into song with "Amazing Grace," it occurred to me that I didn't have the faintest idea how or what kind of cookbook to write.

Research at the library proved discouraging. There were so many kinds and on every possible food and style of eating. I knew also that I would have to be original if I were to have any chance in the publishing industry. The thousand-page writer's manual I had purchased was equally discouraging, predicting that of all manuscripts submitted to publishers, only ten percent ever saw the retail shelf. (I was later told it was more like 0.3 percent.)

To cheer myself, I decided to browse the shopping mall (a stay-at-home mother's favorite pastime). Wandering about, I began to notice all sorts of people carrying little boxes of muffins, freshly bought at MMMMuffin outlets. Sixty-five cents a piece! I could not believe the price but developed a craving nonetheless. I baked my own when I returned home.

After the children were in bed, I had tea with a muffin. Still racking my brain for a good cookbook concept, I mused over the muffin phenomenon. Even in shopping centers, people now seemed to prefer eating muffins to donuts, I thought. Again, I experienced that inner twinge when my intuition tells me something feels right. The feeling became stronger. Of course — muffins!

The idea for my cookbook was born. It was as simple as that. How many recipes could I invent? Fifty muffins would make a very slim book; one hundred sounded better. I announced the project to David. ("Are you really serious?" he asked. "One hundred different kinds of muffins?!")

The next morning I began baking with a purpose. I became a woman obsessed with muffins. Disposing of the "rejects" became a problem as plastic bags full of muffins accumulated in my chest freezer. My sister Karen took them to the crew in the office; my girlfriend with the seven school-age children took them for lunches and I gave my parents the ones I was too ashamed to give to anyone else. My family, of course, ate a lot of muffins. Annie, who was only four months old when I started baking, never experienced Pablum — cream-of-wheat muffin bits became her breakfast and squash muffins, her dinner. What my family couldn't manage went into our giant bird house; the flock grew as they spread the word. I finally let up when I had developed 150 varieties.

Having questioned career and motherhood, I had turned a significant page in my life and come to a solution tailor-made for me. My self-development thus far had been hard work but had also uncovered some surprising rewards; I became a published cookbook author in the process.

Filling The Mastery And Pleasure Cups

I have since come to understand this passage of my growth very clearly. Just as Gail Sheehy presented me with new insights, so I also gained much from the three women who authored *Lifeprints*. Baruch, Barnett and Rivers have written an interesting thesis on the concepts of *mastery* and *pleasure*. They taught me that in order for me to have a total feeling of well-being, I must balance and satisfy these two components within me. *Mastery* I achieve from the feelings of self-esteem and control in my work. *Pleasure* I achieve from feelings of contentment and optimism found in marriage, children and sexuality. Success in both of these dimensions, and hopefully a nice balance of the two, will give me a holistic sense of well-being. So as not to confuse our intuitive understanding of the words "mastery" and "pleasure," here is an illustration.

In *Somebody Has To Do It*, Penny Kome observed that homemakers achieve feelings of total well-being when involving themselves in interests outside of the family. In terms of *mastery* and *pleasure:* a woman mends for her family, but once she decides to use that skill "creatively" to satisfy the self, she will achieve the self-esteem that comes from the mastery side of her. Women who are skilled at crafts and who sell them at bazaars are women who have satisfied themselves on the mastery level. Thus, skills which have traditionally been associated with family (the pleasure component) have been made into small "cottage industry" businesses and given many homemakers success on a mastery level. Had I taken my pottery more seriously, I might have decreased my frustration. As it was, I came to view working on the wheel as I did housework, that is, all that clean-up for a little shine. I think it is crucial to understand that our attitude is at the core of what invariably falls into the mastery/pleasure categories for each of us.

Gail Sheehy's *Passages* enabled me to see that I was paying too little attention to some sort of work of my own outside of the family. In light of *pleasure* and *mastery* all of my energies were being poured into the pleasure dimension of my life: stepchildren, David, cooking, parents, pregnancies. As I isolated myself further, my self-esteem fell. With the passing of time, my mastery dimension needed attention. With Annie's birth, I was already coming to recognize that I needed some sort of work in my life. But staying home with my children was equally important to me. I felt I had no choice but to place my other needs related to mastery on the back burner until Annie went to school. Sheehy helped me to understand that this sacrifice was neither necessary nor good for my creative well-being.

I believe that there were periods for Heather when she was dealing with the same mastery/pleasure balance, but from the other side of the fence. As a full-time working mother, she had known for years that she was competent in her job. Her responsibilities, position and salary increased proportionately. Her "mastery cup" was full. To fill her "pleasure cup," Heather painted ceramics, read, did needlepoint, as well as having her children and long-time male companion. It is my personal view that Heather's children, who would often give her much joy on the "pleasure" level, also challenged her "mastery" as it may have also at times felt like a full-time "job" when as a single parent she had little male support in her household.

Over the years, however, she managed beautifully until she, too, arrived at a new passage and ended the relationship with her long-term companion. The home she had tastefully decorated needed to be sold for a smaller condominium in an area where she had no wish to relocate. Over-burdened with new financial, as well as family adjustments, Heather's pleasure cup seemed close to empty. I bring this up to emphasize that, despite our best efforts, each of us at times become depleted and out of balance; the grass may look greener on occasion, but ultimately I have to fill the same cups that Heather does.

I believe that most women intuitively search for ways to round out their lives by incorporating various interests into them. It is suggested by the authors of *Lifeprints* that these interests involve something totally different than what is usually done in the home. For example, if it's housework you need to get away from, then don't take a job for a housekeeping service. A library, a flower shop, or a cosmetic counter are all better alternatives. Similarly, volunteer for positions which utilize other skills besides domestic ones. Too much of anything can become wearisome. While writing the muffin cookbook, I stopped baking for fun. Unfortunately, this meant that over and above the barrage of muffins, we now had no more quiche or homemade chicken pot pies in the freezer.

There is no question that a full-time homemaker has enough expertise and skill to more than help her achieve satisfaction on the mastery level. Her situation is such, however, that she does not get reimbursement, and sadly, in this world, when no income is attached to one's abilities, the energy is devalued. Society still reinforces this attitude by placing women firmly in the home and enforcing their role as nurturer and "chief cook and bottle washer." Many men are still loathe to share equally in household tasks. According to Penny Kome's survey, a working woman still feels she comes home to her second job. It is little consolation to know that what you do in the home is worth $20,000 per annum if your husband had to replace you. Even if he did pay you $20,000, would you ultimately feel satisfied? Would you feel successful on the mastery level? I think not. I compare this to the many years I worked for my mother after school in the store. She wasn't going to fire me on the days I didn't give 100% to the job (she needed me too much), and the money she paid me didn't feel nearly as good as when the Department of Recreation paid me for camp counseling the following summer.

Having established that finding work of value outside the home increases a woman's inner harmony, then it is not surprising that studies conducted by the writers of *Lifeprints* showed that working mothers were, on the whole, the most satisfied and best balanced with their mastery and pleasure.

Out-Of-Step-Anxiety

When I left the workplace to raise children, I found the adjustment enormous. (Why not? Men are expected to have problems when they retire.) Three years later, when I felt unfulfilled, I thought there was something wrong with me. I had been conditioned to think that a woman should be able to find complete happiness in her home.

This conditioning creates what the authors of *Lifeprints* call *out-of-step-anxiety* which simply means that if a mother works when she doesn't have to, she steps out of line with what society dictates as "right" or "good." Then what of women who enjoy working for its own sake?

In *Outrageous Acts and Everyday Rebellions*, Gloria Steinem makes reference to those mothers who may not need to work for economic survival, but enjoy working and are afraid to admit they actually love and want to work. They justify working by setting up circumstances for themselves to demonstrate to the world and to their families that they *must* work. "If you can manage it, stay at home with your children" is still society's strong message.

For my mother's generation, the message might be "If you can, also help your children with their children, and be a *good* grandmother." I see this as a continual source of self-doubt and anxiety for my mother. She helps us frequently, but still loves to work as well. As she nears retirement age, Mom gives herself external reasons (a large new purchase, three insurance bills at once) to keep working a little longer. The truth is she loves how working makes her feel, despite the weariness of the pace. Her guilt makes her vulnerable to comments made by her family. My father, who has come to understand this, now encourages her to work, and his support in this regard is very important to her. The authors of *Lifeprints* confirm this; those women vulnerable to the out-of-step syndrome often look to their mates for approval. Furthermore, findings have verified that women on the whole put greater weight on how their decision impacts the family than men do. As a result, my mother has sporatic non-working periods until the desire to get back into the thrust of business becomes too much for her, and she realizes she's no better for her family when home full-time.

Societal Conditioning: The Shoulds

It doesn't seem fair that many men can make career decisions unburdened by domestic expectations or what other family members desire. From boyhood, a man has been conditioned to aggressively go after whatever is necessary to further his career. A young girl is conditioned to nurture and place her needs second to home and family. These attitudes are seen time and time again in small but significant way such as a mother who wears the same winter coat for ten seasons while her adolescent daughter has the trendiest items. It is still a virtue for a woman to make sacrifices for her family.

It always astounded me how David could sleep soundly through the baby's crying in the night. I was seriously concerned that he would not awaken in an emergency if I were away. When I began to take trips out of town, I asked him if he had heard Annie cry. "Of course," he replied. "When you are not there, I'm always ready to jump up. I even sleep less deeply because I know I have to do it." I realized then how well I had conditioned him to rely on me. He was the working man after all, and I had made the appropriate sacrifices by always getting up in the night. What else have I been unknowingly teaching my daughter?

The ultimate freedom is to work because you want to, stay home because you truly enjoy it or, as in my case, find work you love to do at home. Whether working, staying home, or both, it is impossible to enjoy it every moment. As long as you would rather not trade roles with another when your imagination gives you the choice, you are probably just where you should be. If, on the other hand, you are contorting yourself in every which way to

do right by your children and family, not only are you
harming yourself, but you are setting yourself up as a
poor role model for them to follow. In many ways, your
child's ability to mother will be learned from you. The
interesting exception to this rule of thumb is the child
who doesn't like what she sees in her mother and learns
by using Mom as an *anti-role model*. I am thinking of a
friend's daughter who was so affected by her mother's
pessimism she became a Pollyanna.

What happens when your consciousness does shift and
it's time to implement changes? Wanting to and going about
it are two different things entirely. Sandra Winston, author
of *The Entrepreneurial Woman*, has some very sound advice
to give on building confidence and changing your direction.

In order to gain better control of our lives, Winston
instructs us to make a list of "shoulds." These are all the
things which have molded your thinking since childhood
and have also, on many occasions, kept you from taking
risks. For example, "A good wife, nice girl, good stepmother wouldn't do that," you may have said to yourself.
In Winston's view, it's time to separate the shoulds into
those shoulds you *want* to do and those you definitely *don't
want* to do.

Being asked to do something and declining because you
don't want to do it is one thing; having always done something and not wanting to do it anymore is a hurdle indeed.
So it was the summer after the memorable Coboconk
fishing holiday. On this point I was clear: I simply did not
want to holiday with four little children for a time, and I
didn't feel I should. While holidays together had strengthened the bond between all of us in the past (especially the
children) and given David extended time with Elizabeth
and Robert, now I also felt it was important to have a
holiday in which I could fully let my hair down. Our
children went to bed much earlier and I yearned for some
private time with David. With two little ones, the pace
was less hectic and I could discipline more effectively. As
far as discipline and holidays were concerned, I could

never bring myself to yell at my stepchildren, even when I wanted to, so I yelled at my own kids instead.

As always, the decisive action I took after that summer had its price, and that price was guilt. Were it not for my feelings, David would have continued as he had done thus far.

Even the most wished-for outcome has its price. My decision to write a cookbook, and the priorities I had to set to keep up the self-imposed schedule of my project, had everyone in my family facing the reality of the price I was willing to pay: higher food costs for ingredients, late nights at the typewriter, mounds of dishes, a limited social life and other laborious tasks.

That year proved to be a personal turning point for me. I dwelt very little now on the issue of self-fulfillment. I was simply doing it. As I researched how to compile a publisher's proposal or write a query letter, I worried less about how well I was dealing with my children and more about how to organize everything I wanted to do. Elizabeth and Robert still came for weekends. Instead of my asking myself what sort of home-baked cookie to have on hand, they were simply offered the "muffin of the day." I "mother-henned" everyone much less, which was perhaps a good thing after all, and I had begun to free myself emotionally from identifying too much with my family.

Finally, the manuscript was complete. I did feel the sense of accomplishment one gets from one's work. In fact, when I sent my proposals off by registered mail, I shed a tear for the entire experience. At that moment, acceptance mattered less than the knowledge that I, who had quit accordion lessons just before I became really good, who had quit my studies when I had really intended to get my Masters, had finally stuck with, and finished, a major labor of love equal in content to any thesis. I was very pleased with myself.

My manuscript came under the scrutiny of several publishers. One was especially interested, and I almost died a thousand deaths when they requested I bake five different muffins in their test kitchen. Finally, there was an offer.

The experience of being assigned an editor, taking part in the promotion and publicity — all were very exciting for a homemaker who had overthrown the family status quo to find a creative outlet for herself. My mastery cup had at last been filled, and I wanted to keep it that way.

6

Acceptance And Stepteens

Even a clock that is not working is right twice a day.
                                                    Polish Proverb

In the three years which followed, the rhythm of our family life shifted to a busy but satisfying pace. I had learned to fill my mastery and pleasure cups and continued to absorb myself in cookbook projects. My muffin book had been launched and promoted, with much excitement for our family, and was selling successfully. Meanwhile, I was up to my elbows in Cheddar cheese, preparing for *Mad About Cheddar*. I grated and melted my way through two hundred pounds of it, and although I found it too much, Elizabeth and Robert seemed to get into the spirit of my experimental recipes. My Cauliflower Cheddar Soup became Elizabeth's favorite.

My stepchildren had arrived at that nice preteen stage when children discover that there are adults around who do "neat" things. Suddenly as a recipe inventor who got to go on radio to talk about her book, I fell into this category. The older children were especially enthusiastic about my new children's cookbook, where they would appear on the cover. Not only had the quality of our snacks upgraded to homemade Fig Newtons, and kids' pizzas, but all the children now felt intimately involved in my work. Adam and Annie were oblivious to the significance of what I was trying to accomplish, but Elizabeth and Robert willingly gave me the leeway to work creatively at my food during their visits with us. It was at this point in our family life that I found my stepchildren most helpful with Adam and Annie. At ages eleven and twelve, they were still pleased with the swims at the local pool and our Saturday night barbecues.

Whatever Heather thought of our lifestyle was unknown to me, as she and I had little contact during this period. I know that I felt awkward about asking her to get Robert's hair cut for the cover of the book. Any promotion for *Fun in the Kitchen* would have meant making arrangements with Heather to remove the children from the classroom, working out their transportation from out of town to our home, and possibly overnight visits on school nights. I opted not to involve them as much as they might have liked. Robert openly told me afterwards that the only time he had ever been envious of Adam was the time he got to appear on "Live it Up," and Robert hadn't. In light of Robert's ability to be very funny, he would have enjoyed it tremendously. I regretted my decision once he shared his feelings with me.

Having now written three cookbooks in three years, my food activities came to a grinding halt. I was burnedout and felt the need to re-direct my energies.

The Status-Quo Shifts

Elizabeth was becoming very excited about her eighth grade graduation from Christian school, and David and I were invited to the banquet along with Heather and her new housemate, John. Another shift was taking place, but this time in Heather's family. David's children now had a new stepfather who was bringing new influences into their lives. I was dying to meet him.

The last time I had been with Heather's family was on the occasion of that awkward Christmas buffet eight years earlier. This time, however, was an entirely different experience for me. I actually enjoyed myself. We had left Adam and Annie behind as they were not able to attend the dinner.

In order to visualize our evening, picture a small gymnasium in a small, fundamentalist Christian school with a strong committee of mothers who had taken great care in producing a personal "food that schmecks" buffet for the graduating class. After several speeches, each graduate was asked to escort his or her parents to the buffet table. One by one, excited young kids stood up to lead their mothers and fathers. Elizabeth was the only child who stood up with *four* adults. Although I felt okay about it, I couldn't help but think about the day several years before when she had confided her wish for a "normal" family life like her friends. Well, she was with her friends now, and I wondered what her thoughts were as the four of us filed behind her to be served. It was clear that this school existed in its own protective bubble.

That bubble would soon burst. Elizabeth and Robert were about to make the transition to the regular public school system close to home. With one year left to complete, Heather and John had decided to remove Robert from his Christian surroundings so that he could be a companion for Elizabeth after school while the adults were at work. As much as he would not have the benefit of graduating with his classmates, the move would also save Robert an hour's transit time alone on the bus, something he and Elizabeth had done together in the past. Elizabeth was eager and excited for these new changes in her life but Robert was worried.

I heaped my plate enthusiastically and devoted myself to the wonderful food as David and John began to discuss Robert's ability to handle the school transition. As I listened to David contradict John I could feel this was a new experience for him. John clearly felt that he knew Robert as well or better than David, and the topic politely shifted

to Robert and hockey. At last Robert had become involved
in his favorite sport. It had always been his dream to do
so, but Heather could not have managed the commitment
to the countless early and after-school practices nor the
transportation it involved. Luckily for Robert, John had
been a player close to "pro" standards. Because he was
small for his age, Heather had always been concerned
about hockey and violence but David's son was spunky,
and John recognized this and encouraged him.

I noticed, however, that even with the discussion on
hockey, David was choosing his words cautiously. He had
also been quite a hockey star in younger years and was as
good a player as John. Well, a little cooperation/competi-
tion conflict never hurt anyone. Welcome to the feeling,
David, I thought.

Whether Elizabeth and Robert were getting older, or
had suddenly been displaced from their conservative private school surroundings, they were changing.

The changes were small at first, and most noticeable
with Elizabeth. It was Annie who first voiced the complaint, "Elizabeth won't play with me anymore." The *Barbie
days* were over, and there was very little we could do. I
took Elizabeth aside and asked her to give Annie a little
time, because as a five year old, she couldn't understand
why Robert spent hours with Adam while she had no one.
Elizabeth gave it her best shot, but was openly bored. The
part of me that could relate to teens understood that going
shopping was more appealing. My heart bled for Annie
though, who idolized her older sister and followed her
around, asking, "Can we play?" The answer was always,
"Maybe later." Annie finally got wise to the fact that her
sister wasn't interested in her as much these days, and that
really hurt. Soon after, Annie began to hang around the
boys, hoping they would include her. Adam wasn't interested but Robert would make allowances.

Robert was not without his influence either. Adam,
who was now nearing nine, wanted desperately to be like
his older brother. Robert had thick brown waves that

parted at the center and a nape of long hair. How could it be that Adam hoped to get his straight, blond, side-parted mop into the same style? There was also the matter of my son's striped polo shirts; Robert wore very long white T-shirts with rock stars imprinted on his chest. I was suddenly dealing with a nine-year-old preteen who saw only the fact that "Robert could do it."

My family had always thought of Elizabeth as a quiet girl, polite, good, feminine, helpful. In many ways she was like her father, quiet but always thinking. From what I knew about quiet children (my sister Karen was labeled one), they had a different side to them entirely, especially when outside the family circle. Quiet girls are often attracted to gregarious, bold girlfriends, who in turn need to be admired by quiet girls. It was no surprise to me, then, when Elizabeth started talking a lot about her "punk" friend, Aster, with the glitzy blouses, spiked hair and loud boots. "I'm completely different when I'm with Aster, you know," Elizabeth told me, and I believed her.

My stepdaughter, who just months before had graduated in a sweet pink lace gown, hand-sewn by her Nan, had made the metamorphosis into a full-fledged high school teen. With her "coming-out," we experienced a different Elizabeth (at least it seemed more dramatic to us, as we saw her much less). I had forgotten what my sisters and I had been like as teenagers and still wonder at my own stupidity of being surprised to discover that Elizabeth had become a sometimes moody, non-participating family member. The make-up, change in hair and interest in boys wasn't what set me back — it was her ability to remain horizontal on the living room couch while I had kitchen duty. Clearly, I was in the "mother mode." Had this been *my* teen, I likely would have insisted on more help. My error again; I was now treating her like a visting stepdaughter.

My ten-year relationship with Elizabeth had regressed to a point where I was not only unsure of what was going through her mind much of the time, but also what she thought of me and our life. This new phase within our blended family taught me several important lessons, including a need for acceptance and tolerance of what teens, particularly stepteens, are all about. Primarily I had "unlearned" two vital truths: that young people who become older essentially crave two things in life, excitement and freedom. As much as Elizabeth and Robert wanted to see us, hanging around suburbia doing what we thought was good fun didn't give them either. Friday evening videos with popcorn, barbecues and bike rides were the little rituals that David and I felt comfortable with. Elizabeth and Robert were growing and "outgrowing." Robert became more involved with his new stepfather, hockey and weekend friends, and Elizabeth acquired a job as stockgirl in a shopping center. Her ambition now was to make enough money for a summer away in England. It was just the change she yearned for after many holidays spent with us and with her Nan and Grandad at the cottage.

It seemed as if a pulling away from us was inevitable. David decided to reassure his children that if they needed to do "their thing" more on weekends, he would understand. Whenever they wished to come, even sporadically, that would be all right with us.

The Boomerang Effect Of Honesty

Sadly for us all, it was at this crucial juncture that we experienced our first major fight with Elizabeth and Robert, and I was the catalyst. During an incident which made me angry, I communicated my feelings for the first time, honestly and directly, instead of venting my frustration to David as I might have done. It was an emotional outburst in which everyone felt involved, and although Adam and Annie had witnessed this sort of openness before, Elizabeth and Robert were shocked.

Outbursts between parents and teens are a fact of life, but they had rarely occurred at our house. Whereas mothers and fathers usually express pleasure as well as criticism, I noticed over a period of years that David was reluctant to say anything negative to Elizabeth and Robert. I know this was in part because, as an absent father, he didn't wish to interfere with Heather's parenting decisions. He was also very aware that his children had a relationship with Heather's companion. Essentially though, in all issues related to "feelings," David simply wasn't the type to be as communicative as some fathers. As much as he was always loving and consistent, he had little desire to stimulate discussions involving growing pains, family conflicts or school pressures. This is not to say that if his children had come to him with these concerns, he would not have expressed his views or given support. It has been my experience that whenever I have been willing to share fears and problems with a child, the relationship automatically shifted to a more initimate level. That has always come more easily to me than to David.

The reason is, of course, because I came from an open, emotional parental home, and David did not. We are all, to some degree, products of our childhood and, on this point, Adam and Annie had parents who communicated quite differently. To my dismay, however, I've often noticed that although David was the father of all four children, he has taken a stronger stand in discipline and criticism with Annie and Adam simply because he lived with them. I understood his need to make the few quality hours with his older children pleasant so they would leave him with good feelings, but I also wonder if he may have denied them the opportunity to see the whole man. In ten years of visitation, when no one had really "let it all hang out," how could David's kids show us all aspects of themselves? Are blended families too busy being on their best behavior?

Most stepmothers certainly try to be. I was so aware that I was a part of the "package deal." Elizabeth and Robert had no choice about that but I preferred to repress petty things which irritated me rather than spoil their weekend. But even that effort is self-deception. Children feel tension regardless; and it's worse if they don't understand it.

The boomerang effect of my honesty occurred when we were given the same back. Several weeks later we were told that the atmosphere in our house was unpleasant and that visitations would stop for a time. Despite the fact that we were long overdue for some thinking about what each of us needed from the blended family, I still internalized David's hurt reaction and Adam's and Annie's confusion, and felt responsible.

Had our weekends together continued as before, it would have given us the chance to work on our problems and get past the tension. Family disputes are normal, I reasoned, and as a blended family we were no exception. What I had to accept was that not everyone deals with conflict in the same way. I also needed to respect Elizabeth and Robert's wishes to separate themselves from us and the problems we represented for them.

Adam and Annie had more difficulty in understanding what was happening and felt suddenly cut-off from their stepsiblings. No amount of explanation about teens being busy and needing more freedom satisfied them. They felt abandoned and related their abandonment solely to the one incident which had triggered the separation.

Finally David questioned his children, "Are you planning to see us sometime soon in the future?" Along with "I don't know," they responded with the remark, "What are we supposed to do, feel guilty?" Clearly they wanted more time.

Elizabeth did go to England, and Robert graduated from public grade school. This time we were not invited for the parent/grad dinner. The school was too large to accommodate extra couples we were told. Instead we sent a silver arm chain with our love and congratulations. And that was the turning point for Robert. He worked with his father part-time in the summer, and to everyone's delight, spent a weekend with us thereafter. Elizabeth, too, had mellowed, but still worked weekends and chose to stay at home.

The passage of time eventually made everything all right. By the time we all came together again as a complete group, Elizabeth and Robert genuinely had a lot of news to share with us. Each one of us had grown in acceptance and appreciation of the varied personalities within our family circle. There was less need to withhold and more desire for openness. What seemed most clear to me was that in addition to Elizabeth's and Robert's special relationship with their father, they also cared about their "package deal" as well.

Stepteens: Letting Go

The letting-go process had felt for a time like an "ungluing" of our entire blended family. The strength, however, which had been established in earlier years, had not been lost altogether. The positive change was simply that in the future we required less "shoulds" and more freedom.

Unfortunately, when parents or stepparents and their children make the transition together into the teen years, they can be each other's worst critics; neither adult nor child seems to satisfy the wishes of the other. It is a phase in which everyone seems to be watching one another more than participating in one another's lives, partially because teens need to test their identity outside the family circle.

I am coming to understand that we are mirrors for each other. My children's behavior always shows me something about mine. And if the reflection is sometimes negative, then on some level, there is always a lesson in it for me. In retrospect, the times I have reacted the most are those in which I have recognized in my child or stepchild a quality which I'm struggling with myself. Finally I have had to acknowledge to myself that the over-protective, limiting attitudes, which I criticized my parents for years ago, are similar to ones I have been inclined to repeat with my own family. Some of the patterns of my childhood have repeated themselves throughout my adult life, creating a *cause and effect cycle* with an all too familiar ring. In this way the old adage, *What goes around comes around*, applies to family life.

Looking Back On What Was Good

In the natural self-scrutiny that most parents go through, a positive way to gain some clarity and balance is to focus on those things, attitudes or actions which were constructive, not destructive. When divorce forces you to re-align your life, the negatives always surface first. However, the positives also need to be acknowledged. Give yourself credit for what you did right.

Here are some of the good things I focused on when I was otherwise discouraged with my life within the blended family.

1. Friends Helped, Not Hindered

As it worked out, neither David nor I brought a large circle of friends with us into our relationship. This meant that, from my standpoint as second wife, I was spared the scrutiny and comparisons some women are subject to. I did not have to establish associations with women who were already well acquainted with Heather and would possibly continue seeing us both, a situation which leaves a second or first wife more vulnerable to the pipeline and often leaves the former couple's personal friends with feelings of split loyalty. It seemed to David and I as if we were starting fresh with the real potential of new beginnings.

2. No Ghosts

Neither of us moved into a home that had been established by the other and the former mate. Thus, we did not have to concern ourselves with former neighbors, mementos, an ex-spouse's house decor, or "the cat she left behind."

3. No Serious Money Problems

We had no serious financial worries, not enough money to splurge on dining out or exotic get-aways, but enough to purchase a modest home and start having fun at local auctions.

4. I Was Just "Angie"

I did not expect to give or receive love instantly with Elizabeth and Robert. From the start, I was Angie, Dad's friend. Naturally, I wished for them to like me and because they were young, found that silly games worked to win them over. I was lucky to have met Elizabeth and Robert when they were younger. Older children would not have necessarily been impressed. When David and I married, I did not expect my role to change in the children's eyes. I remained Angie. My research confirmed that children resent having to call a stepmother "Mom," even when the biological mother is absent. Findings also show that the relationship between children and their stepmother develops slowly, although younger children are more apt to show early warmth and need for affection.

5. Respecting Physical Intimacy

When I met David I discovered that Elizabeth very much enjoyed cuddling with her father and, on our first day-trip as a foursome, she reacted negatively each time he took my hand or demonstrated any physical affection. Sensitive to this, David and I agreed not to embrace or walk holding hands. In this way, the children became accustomed to me as a fun person who had come along with Dad for the day, and any physical expression of affection was intoduced later — slowly.

6. Letting David Be Dad

David did not interfere in my relationship with his children, and whenever I did take a stand, he always backed up my authority. The children, knowing this, never played manipulative games such as asking permission from one adult, knowing the other would say no. Whatever David and I did agree upon, we worked out privately. My reading brought to light the finding that the less a father interferes with his companion or new wife, the greater the chance closeness will develop between her and his children. Some custodial parents, influenced by the guilt they feel toward their children, become over-protective. Quarreling over the children will create tremendous feelings of conflict and guilt for the biological parent, who then finds his loyalties split.

7. Sensitive Disciplining

As a weekend stepmother, I did not wish to correct Elizabeth's and Robert's behavior. Children are already accustomed to parents nagging about manners. Professionals, however, recommend dealing directly with children for open and honest communication. Whether rightly or wrongly, on this point, I chose to disregard their advice. If something Elizabeth and Robert did bothered me, I usually had two approaches:

(a) I would wait for my own children to make the error which irked me, correct Adam and Annie and hope the older ones would catch on. This often worked. Telling Adam to remove his elbows from the table invariably caused the other children to check their elbows.

(b) I would ask David to help correct something. Coming from a father, I felt the criticism would be more easily accepted. David was usually willing to act on my suggestion because I came to him infrequently.

Each parent has his own "bug-bears" and code of etiquette. David, as a father, has the right to decide what he might wish to enforce. Heather has her own attitudes about manners and what she considers important. In our family, there has always been the understanding that Elizabeth and Robert observe our rules when with us, Heather's rules when at home. In terms of manners, I have my own ideas on what is important; however, I am still reluctant to impose my standards on Elizabeth and Robert. For example, in our household we use our knife and fork in the continental way (i.e., never put down the knife or interchange knife and fork between hands). Elizabeth and Robert eat differently. It would not be fair to make them eat awkwardly when Heather uses her cutlery in the North American way.

Feelings about social and table manners are quite another issue if the children live with the stepmother. Pre-adolescent stepchildren might react to frequent nagging with the classic line, "You can't tell me what to do — you're not my mother!" Inappropriate behavior can only be changed if adults show patience and sensitivity, a great deal of which depends on your tone of voice and body posture.

8. Love And Loyalties

David and Heather never made the children feel that their loyalties were split or in question. If one parent is against the other and looks to the child for sympathy, the child who loves *both* parents feels torn. Visitation becomes strained and anxiety builds up within the child who has to account to the custodial parent and possibly cover up for the other. This has been referred to as *the wish-bone effect*. Being pulled and torn and stretched between parents is one of the most difficult experiences a child of divorce will ever encounter. This wish-bone effect can also come about when there is a high degree of competition between ex-wife and stepmother. A child may learn to keep shared experiences with the stepmother to himself or herself, having learned that after weekend visits Mother has reacted with jealousy.

9. Refusing To Compete

David did not allow himself to compete with any companion Heather formed a relationship with. If the children came for the weekend and made reference to another man who had taken their mother and them someplace, David did not become defensive. Nor did he pry or question them regarding their feelings toward him. Frequent rivalry can occur between the biological father and new companion or stepfather. When the child's mother remarries, her new husband should have the freedom to demonstrate authority, to discipline his stepchild, as well as demonstrate affection. If comparisons are constantly made between the new father's way of parenting and the biological father's, a long-lasting competition can be established.

10. No Preconditions

Once having established my relationship with David, Heather allowed David and me 50/50 authority during the period of time I shared with Elizabeth and Robert. There were no lists of *do's* and *don'ts* while the children visited. As an ex-wife, Heather understood that for the sake of the children it would be better for her to relinquish her authority as biological mother so that we could all have maximum enjoyment from the visits while Elizabeth and Robert became a part of our household. I very much appreciated this attitude.

11. Flexibility

Heather allowed a completely flexible visitation pattern. The separation agreement did not stipulate exact intervals. This was a decidedly good thing when we were in stages of transition, moving from one town to another, or adjusting to the birth of a child. Conversely, without rigid structure, and with our lives being as busy as they were, it was sometimes easy to let five or six weeks elapse between visits. There were no real complaints voiced. In the early years, we partially made up for this by sharing our vacations with Elizabeth and Robert. As the children grew older and joint vacations stopped, we established a bi-monthly pattern for a time with the understanding that, even within this arrangement, there was flexibility.

12. No Backbiting!

The adults did not discredit each other in the eyes of the children. It would be silly to pretend that there were not times when David and I would privately discuss Heather or areas of the children's lives. It is human nature to believe that *we* could make improvements. On weekends when the children described their week-day activities to us, we never outwardly judged or voiced an objection. Obviously, our lifestyle was very different from Heather's. It was very tempting to compare.

13. An Independent Ex

Although Heather remained a single mother, she did not badger David, as some former wives might, with continual child-rearing or financial problems. We realized that

Heather did have her struggles, though, through comments the children sometimes made. I assumed for some time that the children preferred chicken to any other meat, until they enlightened us that they ate so much chicken because it was less expensive than beef. Throughout the various changes of her childrens' school life, as well as coping with two moves, Heather's independence and ability to cope astounded me.

14. "Dealing The Grandparents In"

For the sake of Elizabeth and Robert, and David's parents, I know that Heather maintained a pleasant correspondence with the childrens' grandparents. In the early years, I had difficulty adjusting to this because Elizabeth and Robert had the opportunity see their grandparents when David visited them, and I had no contact with Paul's parents. Later, I came to understand that Heather might wish a relationship with her former in-laws for her own sake.

15. We Are Your Other Family

Elizabeth and Robert have always felt that we are their alternate family. In the event of crisis or tragedy, they have their father's support as well as mine. Children look to parents for expressions of love and security. A few years ago, while we were all in the car, Elizabeth said quite casually, "Mommy told us that if anything happened to her, we would come and live with you." We responded immediately with "Of course, we're your other family." That was all that was really needed. Elizabeth and Robert just needed the reassurance of hearing what they already felt to be true, and the issue was laid to rest.

16. A Strong Family Circle

Heather was able to give her children a strong intimate inner family circle. Within their own household, Elizabeth and Robert had relationships with their grandparents, uncle, aunts, as well as the support of a "church family" in which Heather was an active member.

17. No Messenger Service

Heather communicated with David directly and in no
way passed messages on through the children. Nor did
she view herself as Elizabeth's and Robert's protector and
speak for the children. An example of this is a mother
telling the custodial father, "Jimmy is afraid to tell you he
doesn't like spinach."

Yo-Yo Emotions

One last word about the emotions which prevail over
us as we struggle to live successfully as a family.

Relationships between members of a blended family or
any family bring with them a complexity of emotions
which can hurt others and confuse us inwardly. How is it
that, at one moment, I am overwhelmed with sisterly love
for Elizabeth as I share dormitory stories with her and
the next day I judge her as insensitive to my feelings?
How is it also that in one year, I have empathetic feelings
for Heather's situation; the next, I find myself feeling
distanced from her? Theodore Isaac Rubin, in his book
Compassion and Self-Hate, writes that very little is wrong
with our yo-yo range of feelings. As human beings, we
are the embodiment of all emotions and a negative emotion can be followed by a positive one. Rubin's viewpoint
is that it frees us up, not only to experience a greater
capacity for and range of emotions, but also helps us to
understand the inconsistencies of others. Again, the tapes
of our past feelings allow us to see others as our mirrors.

The best thing ultimately is not to drag ourselves
through guilt and remorse, but rather to give ourselves
the same compassion we willingly extend to others in the
same circumstances. Our *on-again/off-again emotional system*
should not cause us to judge ourselves as weak or abnor-
mal, for according to Rubin, this is the very affirmation
of our *aliveness*.

PART III:

Letting Go And Letting Live

Breakfast In Bed

On Mothers Day
Oh lucky me
I get a breakfast
Catered free
And while I'm dying
To sleep in
I hear strange sounds
And whisperings
With echoes of
Collective confusion
I lie in my bed
To preserve the illusion
My peace of mind
Is finally shattered
As cupboard doors and pans
Are battered
Until I can hear
Several little feet creeping

So as not to awaken
Dear Mom, who is sleeping

I can see by their faces
They're tickled I'm pleased
With a rose from the garden
And juice that's hand-squeezed
And *egg-thing,* then followed
Unnervingly green
with pride it's announced
Poached Eggs Florentine
I meekly inquired
Why had they forsaken
The tradition of pancakes
With syrup and bacon
"Pancakes are too boring"
I heard them all say
"Dad got the idea to try something gourmet"
With six loving eyes
Glued upon me, I ate
And managed to finish
The entire green plate
Mothers Day was not over
As you may have guessed
Upon entering the kitchen
I had cardiac arrest

Alive and well
I'm here to say
Tradition's back
On Mothers Day
And though my peace of mind's
Still shattered
In retrospect
It hardly matters
The pancakes are the best I've seen
I've lived through
Poached Eggs Florentine!

Angela Neumann Clubb

7

The Child Factor

*No one can make you feel inferior
without your consent.*

Eleanor Roosevelt

Children are a joy — but also a stress. This truth is not fully understood until we actually become parents. The more solid your reasons are for having children, the more resilient you will be when you are challenged; and whatever your initial expectations might have been about remarriage, motherhood and stepmotherhood, they rarely work out exactly the way you had imagined. If you have married a man with children, and the two of you decide to have children, certain conflicts and frustrations are pre-determined.

Research in family studies indicates that children and financial difficulties are the two principal areas to create conflict in second marriages. My own experiences have borne this out. The conclusion to be drawn is that it would be a very good idea to come to know your future stepchildren before you make a commitment to marriage. An instant and mutual dislike between them and you is a bad omen for any couple.

If you have already made this commitment, you might now take the opportunity to evaluate your situation and your role as parent or stepparent. If you have never had a child but are considering one, examining your motives once more is also a good idea. In light of the overwhelming pressure women feel to have children, let's look at the societal "shoulds" first.

Before I had children, I often heard my aunts say that without them my life would have no meaning or purpose. Some went so far as to emphasize that women who choose not to have them are selfish. The *should* and the *guilt* attached to these traditional beliefs are big ones and require serious introspection.

Authors Susan Gettleman and Janet Markowitz defend those women who shy away from children, but also fear the disapproval of their families and community, in their book *The Courage to Divorce*. The writers draw an excellent comparison between a woman's birth "equipment" and her vocal chords. Their point is that, just as every woman with vocal chords is not expected to become an opera singer, so she need not feel obliged to have a child just because she's been given the "equipment" for the task. We have the free choice to use our reproductive organs, if we really desire to.

According to Baruch, Barnett and Rivers' book *Lifeprints*, wrong reasons for choosing to exercise your right to become a mother are:

1. Children will give your life meaning and purpose.
2. You will be lonely, unloved and miserable in later years if you don't have children.
3. You will be a good daughter if you have children.
4. You will not be a real woman without having a baby.
5. A baby will patch up your marriage.

There are, of course, women who have children for just these reasons; some of them have certainly occurred to me during times of my life when I felt non-directional.

The Second Wife Who Wants Children

If you are a second wife, children will magnify your difficulties. Concerns over children create tensions in all marriages, even the best. A second wife must bear in mind that she will naturally wish to favor her own children if a conflict arises between them and her stepchildren. This, in turn, places a strain on her relationship with the father, whose love is equal as far as all of his children are concerned. The tendency in a stepmother to show bias to her own children may cause her to feel guilty and to over-compensate in order to re-establish balance in her mind or make things right.

When Adam and Annie were born, it was very important to me that I show no favoritism while Elizabeth and Robert were with us. I bent over backwards to be fair. What stepmother likes to think of herself as a nasty stereotype? When disputes did occur between my children and stepchildren, I found myself coming down harder on my own two than would have been the case if Elizabeth and Robert had not been present.

Rarely have I raised my voice to Elizabeth and Robert. In contrast, I have had to close the skylight when Adam and Annie made me angry. I pointed this discrepancy out to Elizabeth one day, telling her it was no coincidence. "You're not my daughter so I'm afraid to yell at you like my own," I told her.

As a woman nears thirty, the question of whether or not to have a child becomes particularly pressing. When the biological clock is ticking, nothing is worse for a woman who desperately yearns for a child, except perhaps her fear that she may not be able to conceive at all, once she decides.

A second wife who comes into a marriage with children of her own has numerous problems to face, but the urgency of children is not one of them. For this reason, she can wisely take her time, not only for a lengthy courtship, but also to let her future husband acquaint himself with her children fully before they marry. It would not be wise for her to exaggerate her future mate's qualities to her children; better, to clearly help them understand just how they will fit into her new marriage.

The second wife who cannot conceive children, and has wanted them desperately, is in the most precarious position regarding stepchildren. If she turns her attention, instead, to her husband's children, they may find themselves with one mother too many. This can cause strain between her and the children's father, who may find his authority overruled. Add the biological mother as a factor in this situation, and you have what my divorced friend, Trevor, experienced.

Trevor was caught in the middle when a woman he was seeing decided to mother-hen his eight-year-old daughter. To understand his reaction, it is important to know that Trevor felt so close to his child that he insisted on co-parenting arrangements with his ex-wife. His apartment was located one block from his ex-wife. Since his separation, Trevor had developed a close father/daughter friendship with Helen. He was pleased that she enjoyed going to concerts with him, as well as the usual kid-oriented activities they did together. For a long time Trevor had absorbed himself in his work and daughter. Then he met Sandra. He brought his new friend along to meet Helen and decided a restaurant would seem a comfortable place to start.

The evening was a disaster! His companion took it upon herself to correct Helen's table manners as well as fuss over her non-stop. Trevor and Helen were insulted. Sandra was intruding in the special, "equal/equal" relationship they had established by treating Helen like a little girl needing "mothering." It was an unhappy situation, because while Trevor understood the needs which motivated his friend, he wasn't looking for another mother for his daughter. She already had one.

This was not the case with me when I first met Elizabeth and Robert. My biological clock was also ticking, but as I knew I would likely be able to have children of my own, I showed no interest in over-mothering David's. Heather could have the discipline. I was happy to take the excursions. I do, however, empathize with any woman who desperately yearns for a child. Until the time I actually conceived, I eyed all pregnant women enviously, watching them in shopping malls or grocery stores. And when I did have the opportunity to watch a young mother interact with her child, I mentally placed myself in her position. Career ambitions, trips, as well as luxuries, all fall by the wayside when a woman actively dreams of motherhood.

If this woman falls in love with a man who has children from a former marriage, but who does *not* plan on having more, it is not a good sign. It may become an ongoing issue between them. And if she does succeed in breaking him down and agreeing to a child, what happens when later they find themselves in arguments over that child? Will he remind her at some point that it was only she who wanted motherhood in the first place? Similarly, if she complains about lack of freedom, exhaustion and boredom (especially if she has left the workplace), this mother must live with the reality that a child was, after all, her wish. Her husband will likely give her little emotional support, rationalizing perhaps that he's been through this already, and it's up to her to deal with it now. If he carries this attitude over into the household or child-care, their marriage will probably reach a crisis.

A husband who has fathered children before is one who can be empathized with also. Knowing the realities of child-rearing, he may now be reluctant to begin again and be unwilling to make the small and large sacrifices necessary, especially if he is much older than his new wife. While he may be looking forward to trips, quiet evenings and a larger social life, her interests would now focus around her children.

A new second wife about to decide whether to have a child would be wise to consider, first, the following *wrong* reasons for having one:

1. A child of your own will make him love you more than his first wife.

2. A child of your own will help him get over not being allowed to see his own children.
3. A child of your own will keep him from going to see his children as much.
4. A child of your own will keep him from leaving you.
5. A child of your own will help your parents accept him.
6. A child of your own will help you stop fighting over his children.
7. A child of your own will show his ex that you and he are finally a family.
8. A child of your own means you can stop working.
9. A child of your own will make him stop working so hard and he will be with you in the evenings.

Those second wives who have had children for any one of these, or any other unsound reasons, may have accomplished what they intended to, but their satisfaction is often short-lived. There is no guarantee that children will make a marriage more cohesive emotionally (although many marriages have stayed intact "because of the children.") A friend of mine told me long ago that "children are the ultimate diversion," by which he meant that couples who would otherwise not remain together, ignore their incompatibilities by concentrating on the children. They can spend years having the activities and worries of children in common, and this "diversion" has enabled them to evade their problems as a couple. It's when the children leave the home that they are suddenly forced to think about themselves. What will keep them together now? Often it is the fear of aging — alone.

Motherhood: A Humbling Experience

There is no question that children add another dimension to life, as well as a commitment we cannot turn our backs on. We have no guarantees that they will grow up as we would like them to. Nor is there any guarantee that they will return our love when we are old. Once you have made the choice to become a parent, along with the joy, you ultimately also pay a price. What that price will be and how it will affect your life and marriage is something no one can predict completely in advance. Short of the obvious financial sacrifices and so on, I had no concept of how motherhood would shape my attitudes. I never suspected that I would come to a time in my marriage when I would have to give my needs priority over my role as mother. I had always thought that motherhood would be an "all-inclusive fulfilling role."

Especially as my children became older, I found my role as mother much more frustrating than I could have imagined. I thought it would get easier, but why then the adage "little children, little problems; big children, big problems?" At the same time, becoming a mother has, more than anything else in my life, taught me the lesson of compassion for my own mother. I am less likely to judge her when it feels like such a struggle to live up to my own standards. My friend, Barbara, used to call motherhood one of life's truly "humbling experiences." Indeed.

My passage into motherhood also changed my outlook on other mothers forever. In my pre-child days, Elizabeth and Robert would irritate me in little ways, ways which I came to handle once I had my own little ones. I used to be silently critical of Heather when Elizabeth and Robert told us they often ate packaged soup and toast, canned spaghetti, or microwaved hot dogs. But when I got my own children, I eventually dished out these same quick meals.

I will never forget the hot summer afternoon in downtown Toronto when I took all four children to Anita's apartment to shoot the cover of my children's cookbook. Anita was my publisher's publicist, had no children and no air-conditioning. It couldn't have been worse for cramped conditions mixed with high anticipation. I had baked enough sample recipes for several cookbook covers and "schlepped" them ever-so-carefully to Anita's. The children were bathed and looked perfect — for the first hour! Who could have known it would take two hours to re-arrange the food and set up cameras? Annie was only two years old and wanted to eat non-stop; Elizabeth was concerned about her hair; the boys were restless. A narrow strip of grass divided the street in front of Anita's place. "Why don't the children play on that little knoll of grass?" Anita suggested. My children took one look at the tiny area and looked at her as if she had just stepped out of a *Polka Dot Door* taping.

The photographer, who was also childless, decided after two hours that the shot was too tight, and one child would have to go. It was clear to me, then, that this woman did not have the mentality of a mother! Annie would not have known the difference if I had left her out but *my* mother would have! "To put David's children on the cover of your cookbook and not yours? Never!" And so it went, until we got through the afternoon. Next time I'll ask for illustrations. God knows what Anita thought of my mothering. I let Annie eat herself sick on gingerbread to keep her still. Anita is a mother now and has no doubt discovered that life with children *is* different.

Whether the decision to have children was made consciously or unconsciously, you are now part of a blended family, and if nothing else, it's *not* boring. Whatever your particular circumstances, first visits or weekends together take some getting used to. What to do when they come? How to make them feel more at home and less awkward? Trying too hard doesn't work. You begin to realize that closeness with another woman's children just doesn't come that easily.

Weekend Visits: Activities To Do Together

This portion will concern itself with blended family situations in which stepchildren are part of a visitation arrangement. I could only imagine the difficulties faced by families where two sets of children cohabit, all varying in age. This *Brady Bunch* situation, from what I have heard, is not entirely the situation-comedy it has been made out to be on television. For those of you who live it, you must no doubt have enough material for several books of your own, as do other non-traditional families who deal with foster parenting and adoption. We all cope with what we have been given or chosen. For my part, I will confine my comments to what I know best: my life as a part-time stepmother to Elizabeth and Robert and full-time mother to Adam and Annie.

Stepchildren, as all children, need some time to get a sense of their situation — and of you. It may appear that they are watching you while you busy yourself with chores, and they likely are. In their own ways, they are no doubt trying to figure you out. Some children do this very quietly, discreetly. Others stare intensely. Don't smother them with attention, and they will soon enough make up their minds about you and relate to you.

In the initial phase of living as a blended family, it may be easier to focus on activities rather than discussions. Some activities lend themselves to cooperative play, and by not focusing on any one family member, contribute to a "safe" feeling, particularly if being observed is a worry. Here, too, the emphasis should be on non-competitive activities, especially between stepsiblings. Parents might wish to make an effort to control natural competitive urges within themselves and their children. Later when everyone feels secure in the family circle, a little competition can be fun if positive attitudes to losing have been taught.

Some icebreakers are:

1. Board games: Clue, Monopoly, Risk.
2. Cooperative jigsaw puzzles.
3. Word games: Spill and Spell, Scrabble.
4. Family sports: Cross-country skiing, skating, swimming, mini-golf, bowling.
5. Excursions to local parks, playgrounds, historic sites, museums, zoos.
6. Crafts: Models, collages, clay.

Since visits cannot solely revolve around recreational activities, this is a good time for Dad to make the effort to *wean* his children into household activities. Although there is nothing wrong with a stepmother suggesting the children help out, you may find that, for a time, it is received more favorably when coming from Dad. Some children are so eager to please their parent that they may welcome doing things for Dad:

1. Making Dad's lunches for the week and freezing them.
2. Learning to sew buttons on Dad's shirts, shining his shoes.
3. Errands for Dad: cleaners, hardware store.

If children have been accustomed to doing things for Dad while he was still living with them, it may be especially welcome if their father remembers this and asks for help. Other tasks may be:

1. Walking or bathing the family pet.
2. Raking leaves or shoveling snow with Dad.
3. Sorting out the workshop or garage.
4. Washing Dad's car.

When your stepchildren have acclimatized themselves to your household, you as a stepmother may wish to take a more active role in suggesting activities which will contribute to their sense of belonging:

1. Ask your stepchild to answer the phone.
2. Ask your stepchild if he/she would like to come to the library. Arrange for his/her own library card.
3. Suggest baking something for the family and do it together.
4. Plan a birthday celebration for Dad. Make a cake with the children and order in something special, like Chinese food. (If your immediate family celebrates birthdays together, you may decide to have the visiting children celebrate before or after. Dad gets two parties then.)
5. Buy and label toothbrushes to keep in the house for their stay.
6. Let them make up a pantry list of foods they would like to see in your cupboards.

7. Young children love to sort out interesting things. Go through old clothes and make bags for charity. They can play dressup at the same time. It may even begin a special box just for that.

8. Rearrange furniture as a family. Get your stepchildren's input. Have special snacks sitting about, put on some music and make it fun.

9. Let them help you plan a garage sale. Arrange it for a weekend when they are visiting. Children love to sell and enjoy the variety of people who come and go. They may even wish to sell lemonade. You may offer to let them bring some toys they want to sell from home.

10. Suggest they help you plan a weekend menu. Each family member will get one special food that they love during the course of the weekend.

11. Invite a couple over for a late supper, but include your stepchildren in serving and eating the appetizers. Once they have sat with the adults for a time, children often want to go off to another activity.

12. Start a new tradition and have Dad serve dessert with the children while you sit and enjoy.

13. Plan a fun communal meal like Cheddar fondue, which requires family involvement and a lot of shoulder-to-shoulder intimacy. If they like melted cheese, this might be a good way to introduce veggies as dippers to fussy palates.

14. Don't ignore your personal interests while they are with you. Let your stepchildren see another side of you besides "Dad's wife." If you have a potter's wheel, then pot. Play guitar or do the research required in your job. In this way, they will come to know you. If you have a skill which they could try, ask them if they are interested in learning how.

15. Let them help you with the new baby, if they appear interested.

Overcoming Little/Big Issues

Despite our best efforts to keep weekends happy, little issues have a way of becoming bigger in a blended family. Often this is the result of one adult's very personal set of priorities. Your priorities may not always coincide with your husband's, those of your stepchildren, nor their mother. What appears on the *surface* to be a picky irritation is often symbolic of a much larger and deeper issue. Eating, or not eating, leftovers is one such example; and on this point I am biased.

Not only do I believe that leftovers are far more delicious at times than the original dish, but I consider it almost a criminal waste to throw them away. This view is rooted in my childhood, when my father not only made large pots of pea soup (which meant many meals of leftovers), but also was the self-appointed "leftover-eater" for any meal going. My brother-in-law, Kevin, really doesn't like leftovers, which means that on that *little issue*, he is not at all popular with my father. I would be more critical, but my sister, Karen, gives me Kevin's leftovers.

Differences such as this can and do create heartburn for a stepmother. It's not always easy to remember that your husband's children have not been conditioned by you, but rather their father, and most especially their biological mother. So if Dad eats with his nose right in the chicken noodle soup and his children do it too, what's a stepmother to do? They, on the other hand, may be going home and telling their mother that you're one of those crazy recyclers, because you wash out your freezer bags.

Let's return again to my *little issue* of leftovers. You now have two choices as a stepmother: enforce your values on the child or accept his preference. For a woman who has children of her own, it becomes difficult. She is obviously trying to encourage her kids to eat them! The children then become aware of an inconsistency in rules; and you'll hear the complaint, "They don't have to — why do we?" Between these two extremes of enforcement and acceptance, there may be yet another way to examine the issue.

Ask yourself, "How important is this issue to me? How do I feel about this habit, rule, etc.? Is this a priority for me because *that's the way it's always been*, or can I also understand the other side?" Concerning leftovers, I had to ask myself if I had loathed them myself as a child, and had I since been conditioned to believe, as my father did, that a child who refused to eat leftovers was "spoiled" or overindulged by his parents. Many times as parents we either do just as our parents did, or the opposite; but whether we reject certain foods, or choose to duplicate the Christmas tree of our childhood, our action usually symbolizes a value or core belief. If your grievance comes down to principle, then your stepchildren may have to acquiesce to your wishes, at least some of the time.

Ask yourself, "Can this issue be avoided next time?" If leftovers are not something you feel you need fight about, then perhaps when your stepchildren arrive, you can have regular meals, saving the leftovers for the weekday or freezing them. If stepchildren, however, wish to become truly a part of your household, they will eventually need to accept the lesson, "When in Rome . . ." It is to be hoped their mother has encouraged them to try to cooperate.

Try and make your stepchildren understand the way you feel about whatever bothers you. In that way, they are seeing it as a part of who you are and what you stand for. Then explain that every now and again, they may have to do something differently than they are used to at home. Once having reached this understanding, make sure that you do not make them live "your way" every time they come, just to prove a point. Children are very perceptive to a stepparent who clearly bends to their way, too. It comes down to mutual respect.

Whether it is leftovers, television, or participation in chores, these issues all serve to create closeness or alienation. Regardless, a sense of fair play and respect for the house rules in their full-time home is required. No family member should have the feeling that it is always one person who "calls the shots." The list that follows are some little/big issues which you and your mate must eventually either agree on, or at least come to terms with.

1. Curfews/Bedtime

- Are younger children free to go to the park alone? If your stepchildren are allowed more freedom in their home, what are the rules for your own children, as well as for your stepchildren?
- How late can your stepchildren stay up? What about your own children? Are your stepchildren allowed to bring a friend to sleep over?
- Should they have to make their own bed and tidy up their things in your home? And if they don't do this in their own home, will you insist on it in your household?

2. Television/Entertainment/Music

- How much television? How long?
- If they are not censored at home, do you have the right? If your children are much younger, should they watch adult shows?
- Should you pay for videos or ask your stepteens to pay for rental?
- Will two televisions solve most of your problems?
- If your husband wants to talk with his children while they prefer to overdose on TV, do you speak up? And will you say anything if your stepchildren can't detach themselves from their walkmans?

3. Discipline

- As a stepmother, do you have the right to send your husband's children home for misbehavior?
- Will you follow the "wait until your father gets home" rule or deal directly with each incident as it comes up? Is there a discrepancy in the way you discipline your children and your stepchildren? If so, do your children understand why this is so?

- Do you consider your husband too lenient with the children of his former marriage and stricter with the children you have together?
- Can your stepchildren discipline your children? How?

4. Food

- How many sweets are too many?
- What about junk food?
- Do you cater to picky eaters?
- Do you stay silent with a stepchild who overeats?
- Do you stock up the pantry before visitations to cater to the food preferences of your stepchildren?
- Do your stepchildren participate in the preparation of food?
- What are the rules about clean up?
- What are the rules if your stepchildren bring food with them? And what if they give foods you disapprove of to your children?
- Do your stepchildren have to finish what is on their plates? Will you allow your stepchild to have a drink, if it's all right at home?

5. Personal Habits

- Do you correct habits that irritate you (for example, biting nails)?
- Do you enforce tidiness rules when your stepchildren are sloppy?
- Can you expect the same behavior as with your own children, i.e., how far can you go?
- What is your stand on table manners? Do you correct them?
- Do you correct poor grammar, foul language or poor telephone etiquette?
- Do you allow your stepchildren to sleep in until they wish to rise?

6. Other Considerations

- Will you let your stepson/daughter borrow your things?

- Do you let older stepchildren babysit younger step-siblings on weekend visits, or is that weekend solely devoted to spending time with stepchildren?
- Do you entertain friends or family during weekend visitations?
- Do you believe it is good to be open about discussing sex with stepchildren?
- How comfortable are you in showing affection toward your mate in front of your stepchildren?
- Do you lend money to a stepson/daughter if asked?
- Should stepchildren know how much money you contribute toward their support? Do you discuss your financial concerns with your stepchildren?
- Do you lend stepchildren the car?
- Do you have an open-door policy; that is, do you wish your stepchildren to feel they can visit or stay with you at any time?

In my case, many of these little/big issues (and some have serious implications) may not have been discussed between you and your husband before your marriage. Now is the time to come to a clear understanding of just what your views and his are. Where is there room for compromise? For give-and-take on both your parts? Then, as a united front, you can convey (not all at once, of course), what you are all about to the children. Their ages will have a lot to do with how they accept your attitudes and adjust to them. And you in turn must be willing to accept and adjust to much of what they bring with them.

As new guidelines are set for your blended family and a new pattern of living is established, time brings along that which needs to be dealt with, as it becomes important to the family.

Good Parenting/Stepparenting Qualities

Dr. Lee Salk, author of *What Every Child Would Like His Parents to Know about Divorce*, is a professional consultant for custody cases. He writes that the following six qualities are vital to good parenting: acceptance, affection, approval, protection, guidance and discipline.

To believe in these qualities — to demonstrate them consistently — is the challenge. Trying to practice them in stepfamilies is even tougher. Let's consider each quality.

1. Acceptance

Whatever a child is, does, or thinks, the child needs to feel acceptance and belonging within the family. The sense of security the child had before the parents separated, which was *their base of belonging*, is now in jeopardy. Both parents and stepparents must help the child find it again within the blended family. The non-custodial parent can reassure their child that they will always be a part of this parent's life. A child who is too quiet, too good or "perfect," may be afraid that if they act otherwise, they won't be wanted. The polar opposite is the child who misbehaves, demonstrating to their parent or stepparent their need for acceptance and loving attention. As a stepparent, you may invest time and energy and feel that you are getting nowhere. Don't give up; eventually your acceptance over time (and time is the key) will help convince your stepchild that they belong. This will only come about once the child has grown to accept that separateness does not necessarily mean not belonging.

2. Affection

"Don't just tell me, show me" is how the song goes. Insincere gestures and words fool no child; they need real physical indications of loving or friendly feelings. *Friendly feelings* mean just that. As a stepparent you don't have to love your stepchild to give a hug or hold his hand. Initially, demonstrating affection may feel awkward to you. Then say something like "I really feel shy about giving you a hug, but I want to," and then do it almost immediately before both of you feel shy. My experience has been that just admitting my self-consciousness helps me overcome it. And you may be surprised; your stepchild may reciprocate faster than you think.

Once affection has been given, the danger is that it can also be withheld when we're not feeling close. Stepfamilies go through phases where misinterpretations can lead to periods of non-touching. When this happens, there's usually one member who is sensitive to what's going on and compensates with extra demonstrations of affection until feelings are equalized. However, it's always very apparent and a stumbling block to good family feelings. Open communication is really the only way to repair anger.

It is also important to understand that each child not only reacts to physical affection differently, but also demonstrates it in their own way. Elizabeth was happy to hold my hand as we browsed through a shopping center. Robert felt comfortable with brief hello pecks on the cheek. As much as I demonstrate affection easily, I had to remind myself that this was Robert's way and no indication of the degree to which he cared.

3. Approval

Disapproval is not necessarily a bad thing if it is given along with healthy doses of approval. A child needs and should have acknowledgment of their positive behavior, accomplishments and feelings. Non-custodial parents (influenced by guilt) must watch the temptation to show too much approval, to be too accommodating or easy going. Similarly, a stepmother may have a tendency to be overly watchful and critical of a stepchild, mainly because the child is not hers. Therefore, she may not be as easily amused or impressed by the child's efforts or antics. But, approval may be hardest to give when a stepmother herself does not receive it from her stepchild. On this point, I compare it to something I once read about love: "You can only hope to receive about as much as you are willing to give out yourself."

One last important point: the approval that stepsiblings look for from one another. Adam and Annie idolized Elizabeth and Robert and reacted with intense hurt whenever they felt impatience or criticism from the older children. It was for Robert's approval that Adam wanted to grow his hair the same and wear similar clothes. Adam was reluctant to try anything new in front of Robert, out of fear that he might look foolish. Elizabeth and Robert were powerful role-models influencing Adam's and Annie's self-approval or self-esteem.

4. Protection

It is important to make children understand that their safety is always of great concern to you, and as limiting as that may feel to them at times, it also gives them security.

As Elizabeth's and Robert's weekend guardian, I was very conscious of my responsibility for their safety, particularly when David was absent. They did not have the roaming freedom with us as in their own neighborhood; later, when I realized just how street-wise my stepchildren were, I became more lenient. As they got older, I noticed that the more I allowed them to protect Adam and Annie when they went off together, the less reason there was for me to be over-protective. No doubt this also increased Elizabeth and Robert's feelings of acceptance and approval by me.

5. Guidance

Parents give guidance by setting guidelines. In this way, a child has some measure of freedom while still feeling protected.

Stepkids are not necessarily pleased about guidelines which may be imposed on them in one household and not another. The positive effect, however, is that if nothing else, the child does get a clear sense of what you as a parent or stepparent stand for, in terms of values. Good, bad, right or wrong, guidelines serve to give kids direction. It is my bias that extremely rigid guidelines have no place in stepfamilies where so much back-and-forth resiliency is needed. Loving guidelines, however, are necessary to good parenting.

6. Discipline

This is not to be confused with physical punishment. Discipline is action (often interpreted as punishment), but motivated by a desire to give guidance and protection. You teach a child discipline by setting limits when important rules have been violated. It's really an extension of showing love, although your child may not consciously recognize this. Unconsciously, however, they do, which is why "undisciplined," misbehaving children often act out because they desperately needs attention (i.e., love).

In blended family terms, some weekday rules may fall by the wayside during visitation, as exceptions are being made to accommodate stepchildren. To a degree, resiliency is a good thing, especially when it makes the transition from household to household easier. Adam and Annie have come to know that there are certain leniencies they can expect when Elizabeth and Robert come, but that life falls into *our* pattern by Monday.

Discipline is also closely connected to respect. When Heather supports our authority, she is also teaching her children to respect our rules. As a stepmother, for the most part, I have disciplined Elizabeth and Robert only indirectly. Through my active disciplining of Adam and Annie, limits and rules were sometimes set for Elizabeth and Robert as well.

The authors of *The Joys and Sorrows of Parenthood* stress the need for inner flexibility in a good stepparent. Whether the role is adopted full-time or on weekends, the authors believe that a stepparent may cross role boundaries at any given time and become a stepparent, non-parent, and a parent.

Clearly then, our parenting roles within stepfamilies must be both adaptable and well-defined.

Stepfamilies have much to learn from the Kanuri Inuit who seem to have found the answer long ago. These people have integrated stepchildren into their culture with more understanding than we have. It was their sense of kinship that established their concept of a *totally extended family*. Offsprings of *any kind* of marital arrangement are considered siblings to one another. Imagine. Regardless of the form of marriage the Kanuri was once involved with, kinship is permanently established from generation to generation. The lesson to learn from the Kanuri is expressed in this quote:

> *Life can only be understood backwards,*
> *but must be lived forwards.*
>
> Soren Kierkegaard

8

Communicating Honestly

When in doubt, tell the truth.

Mark Twain

While I agree with this maxim in principle, I could not help but be amused with Mark Twain. He was not, I was sure of it, a member of a blended family.

Though truth is a value, an intangible, we human beings give it its energy. Truth then becomes *real*, let us say, like money. Money is simply paper or coins, and as such is meaningless (i.e., neutral) energy, until I give it power. It is the quality and value I attribute to it: what good or bad I accomplish with it, my attachment or willingness to part with it. So it is with truth, which also simply *is;* until I take into account my feelings, motives, how I come across with truth, and other factors which give my honesty energy.

In my understanding of it, the issue of honest communication falls firmly into the shaded gray area of life. For this reason, I tend not to categorize lies into only black or white ones. Instead, I feel that the truth in my life is continually being manipulated and interpreted by my conscious mind. My unconscious *always* has the knowledge of real truth, but I may not always want to listen to it. By the time my conscious self has finished, truth may well have been transformed into what we know as silence, flattery, excuses, half-truths, and yes, white and black lies.

Body Language, Tone And The Words

In communicating our thoughts, findings have shown that all communication is broken down to 55 percent body language, 38 percent tone and only seven percent actual words spoken. Clearly, we impress others not so much by what we say, as how we say it. Criticism, offered lovingly, is another matter entirely. The next time you hear yourself saying, "What did I say?" think again. What was your voice and body expressing? Couples who have been married several years seem to allow themselves tonal and facial expressions which they would not dream of using with their friends.

No wonder, then, that David was surprisingly unoffended when I told him directly but lovingly before we married that I couldn't bear him biting his nails. "You've got such nice looking hands," I remember telling him. "It's such a shame to spoil their look. Please stop!" And he did.

After we were married, I became a good deal more direct in my criticism of his habits. When I questioned him on why he was making no effort to change them, he told me honestly that my tone of voice gave him little motivation to do so and suggested I might try a softer approach. "Can't I be honest?" was my weak retort (knowing full well I was taking our marriage for granted, and wording my criticisms more carefully with friends).

Robert had a similar reaction when his father told him bluntly one weekend to get a haircut. The fact that his hair was too long was obvious to everyone, so also was the disapproval and impatience in David's voice.

If indeed the words we use account for only seven percent of our communication, does that imply that we have the license to say whatever we honestly feel? I think not. Discretion is important when the urge to be honest comes over you. I could have done with a little less honesty the last time Heather and I had tea.

On impulse, I had decided to drive Elizabeth and Robert home on Sunday and let David rest. When I arrived with the four children, Heather was baking cookies for the freezer, by the dozen. In ten years, I had never appeared alone, but she responded warmly, "I'm just making lunchbox treats to tide my family over while I'm away on business next week in Switzerland." I'd bake cookies, too, I thought, if I could leave my family behind for a week and travel to Switzerland. I accepted her offer for tea and parked myself in the corner away from the production line. "Now that you're here," she continued, "there is something I've always wanted to say to you." Here it comes, I thought, she's going to bring up the time Robert got sick for two days on my Cheddar fondue.

"First, I want you to know that in all the years my children have been coming into your home, I really feel you've given them your best efforts, and I thank you for that," Heather said instead.

Frankly I didn't know what to do. It is no doubt the most meaningful thing she will ever say to me. I was touched by her genuine warmth. Very few ex-wives could have come across in this way. To my chagrin, she followed with a flattering remark about my good food over the years. "Every time the kids come home, I get a list of all the interesting dishes you have made."

That did it. She had me in her back pocket for life. We talked about her work and how her life had changed since John had become her housemate six months earlier. Five minutes later, he arrived home, and we were introduced. "John, this is Angie," Heather said. "You see! It *is* possible for a first and second wife to get along!"

That was a loaded comment and, judging from the look on John's face, one with a lot of meaning in their household. We exchanged polite hellos, and John took his cookies and went to the bedroom to watch TV.

Elizabeth had, during our entire conversation, been sitting beside me, keenly listening to our chit-chat. A comment made by Heather about weight drew a comic remark from her daughter about David's extra poundage and "love handles." And that's when Heather spoiled it. "Now listen here, Elizabeth Jane, when *I* married your father, he was quite a catch and very handsome. Thin, sandy-blond hair, nice muscles! He didn't look *then*, the way he looks *now!*"

My God, my little voice was saying, what are you implying? That *you* got the filet, and *I* the chopped liver? Certainly Heather wasn't aware of how her remark had been interpreted by me, but I was insulted for David, as well as myself. She may as well have told her daughter that in their marriage she had enjoyed David in his prime, and I'd gotten him the way he was now. "I like his looks," I said quietly. "He's kind of like a sexy bear now."

If 55 percent of that exchange was body language and 38 percent tone, had Heather noticed that I was suddenly having difficulty swallowing my cookie and my body had shifted from a comfortable slouch to a 45-degree angle?

I've come to the conclusion since that I am far too sensitive about conversations with Heather which allude to the physical intimacy she and David once shared. It had made me just as uncomfortable eight years earlier when in David's presence (and over tea, again), Heather winked at me and made a comment about David's derriere. "We both know he's got big, muscular buns, don't we, Angie?" I felt at that moment as if I were intimately involved in a private joke between us much like two sorority sisters who had dated the same man. At the time, I didn't respond, but we may as well have been locating his mole — I was embarrassed.

Non-Custodial Fathers: Attitudes And Communication

In contrast, David was unaffected by Heather's honesty in both instances, which is just as well, considering his "buns" and his "handles" were the ones under scrutiny.

David's reaction is the crucial other factor and must not be overlooked. I was often astounded at his blase approach to issues which would have disturbed me or others in a similar situation. The most blatant example was when Heather allowed, perhaps even encouraged, her children to call her long-time companion, Greg, "Daddy," even though this man did not live with her family. When I met Elizabeth and Robert, there was "Daddy Greg," and "Daddy David." This distinction had to be made, so as not to confuse their stories, which often began with "When Daddy and I did . . ." by which they meant Daddy Greg.

As David was an active part of their lives and had never been absent from his children for long periods, I found this "two-Daddy thing" puzzling. I felt that it was not only unnecessary (after all, the kids called me Angie), but it also created another loss when Heather and Greg dissolved their relationship. Elizabeth and Robert lost another "Daddy." This mostly affected Robert who had grown more attached to Heather's friend than Elizabeth.

Now, several years later, Heather cohabits with John. The last time I spoke with Robert on the telephone, he told me of their planned trip to Nova Scotia "with Mom and Dad." I couldn't understand how he had come to have two fathers again, at age fourteen. I noticed also that he referred to his stepfather not as Dad, but John, in conversation with David.

Who had encouraged the adoption of the new Dad title, and why was David so surprisingly detached about the matter?

"What good would it do if I said anything?" he answered when I probed his feelings. "Of course, it bothers me."

I concluded that David was more mature than I. And my former companion, Paul, would not have been capable of this. He involved himself intensely with most larger decisions Linda made concerning Brendon. Heated telephone discussions no doubt made her feel as if she was walking on glass.

And that was not good either. For me, Paul and David typify polar opposites in non-custodial fathers. Whereas there was very little in life that Paul *didn't* get intense about, didn't over-analyze or complicate, there was very little that *did* upset David and which he couldn't find a solution for in five minutes.

Neither approach is ideal. David, who is less talkative by nature, often appeared to relate on a more surface level, thus missing out on some very real and meaningful conversations he could have had with his children. Elizabeth articulated this one day when she remarked that she sometimes felt she did not really *know* her father: "He never tells me anything."

For a man like David, communicating honestly becomes even more difficult with the children he's not living with, especially if heart-to-heart discussions are what his kids are hoping for. Although David maintains he enjoys open talks, it does not occur to him to begin one. In light of the sometimes closeted personality of teens and given the fact that Elizabeth is also not usually the open one first (as well as having "girl concerns," which are sometimes awkward to discuss), it is no surprise then that father and daughter have established a binding tie of love, but not necessarily close and honest communication.

Robert, however, is an open, communicative kid, who freely launches into his personal concerns with David. Usually this involves peer problems and his stature. David was able to relate his own experiences to Robert as he, too, had been very short in grade school, and this common problem sparked some very good conversations between them.

Consistent with his personality, David is much the same with Adam and Annie, addressing issues only as they are brought up by them. Perhaps that's all right too, for I'm the one who often anticipates their feelings and I do more than enough worrying and talking.

I come from a household where honesty is very much valued. The unspoken rule, however, which was established in my childhood, is this: Children must above all show respect for their parents. If you are going to be honest, and the truth as you perceive it is negative, then the criticism must be cushioned with lots of good words, so as not to appear unloving or offensive. Certainly I did not heed this wish in my teenage years, as I grew extremely critical of my parents, and often told them straight out how I felt. Once I married, and particularly once I became a mother, I grew to become extremely aware of how I was communicating with them.

As David was a man of few words, he often came across with his opinions a little too harshly. What had just taken me five minutes to express ever so delicately, David did with two words. ("That's crap!" was his favorite.) His manner of communicating was just a little too straightforward and subsequently became a "little/big issue" with my parents, especially my mother. Afterwards, I would often plead with him to modify his communicative technique. "David, family is not the Toronto Food Terminal. As a buyer, it's appropriate for you to curse over a two-cent increase in lettuce!" There, David was known for his efficiency and ability to cut through the social chit-chat and get to the bottom line at once, which was price. Unfortunately, the price at my house was that he was being consistently interpreted as too crass. My Uncle Allan found David refreshingly to the point, but then Uncle Allan had made himself unpopular with family for just the same reasons.

The Active Speaker/Active Listener Balance

My communicative weakness, on the other hand, was a fondness for exaggeration; I would take any opportunity I could get to tell a good story. When I found myself in the company of a good listener, I often got carried away (entertaining myself really) with descriptive anecdotes of my family life. That I should perhaps try to cultivate some listening skills is something that I have consciously had to work at over the years.

This is not to imply that I never listened. I spent several years doing very little else when I was with Paul. Socially, he dominated every conversation. His ego-need to shine was a strong as mine. It is no accident, then, that I gravitated to a man like David who, despite his bluntness, was always my best listener and who consistently provided me with excellent feedback. On this basis our mutual *active speaker/active listener partnership* was established. What sometimes appeared to others as an unequal distribution of "voice" in our marriage more than suited both David and I for a long time. We, after all, had established this status quo.

This was in fact the reverse of the unspoken status quo which had been established in my former relationship with Paul. He had met me as an animated talker. My need to hear his unique views and to learn from his experiences was, for a time, compatible with his need to express them and to influence me. What developed over time was that I remained the extrovert and communicator at work and adopted the role of primary listener and introvert at home. As a result, the basis of our communicative compatibility needed to change. The status quo which had suited me once no longer felt satisfying.

Just as I tired of becoming the primary listener in my former relationship, so I eventually tired of being the primary talker in my relationship with David.

"Let's talk," I would suggest to David. "So talk" was his answer. This response eventually angered and frustrated me and needed to be worked out between us. David had fallen into a comfortable laziness by expecting me to stimulate our discussions.

This brings me to a crucial lesson I have had to learn about communication in all of my relationships: *Regardless under what terms our communication with one another was established, in order for it to stay alive and interesting, we must willingly be able to interchange our roles.* As much as David will essentially remain the introvert in our household, so too does he enjoy taking the lead now and then in active talking. Remember too: *In every primary listener, there also lives the primary talker.*

It is often a question of atmosphere, opportunity and striking the right "communicative chord." When it comes to the subject matter of the produce industry (David's work), as well as fishing and the out-of-doors (David's passion), I have been astounded to notice that my husband, with little more prompting than a genuine well-directed question thrown in his direction, is transformed into a speaker with strong personal views and much to share.

No individual is really boring. If it appears to be so, we must first reserve our judgment until we look at our own ability to communicate *and* listen. It was when I learned to "shut up" long enough to listen, to stop feeling that I had to fill in every group silence, that I became a better communicator and friend.

Coming Across Honestly

Genuine feelings, and the communication of those feelings, are vital in maintaining a positive atmosphere within the blended family. How we are perceived, then, is of utmost importance in establishing this positive atmosphere, and each family member is vulnerable to misinterpretation. It is my belief that honest communication of feelings is only half of it: honest interpretation is the other 50 percent. The most sincere tone and positive body language mean nothing unless the person with whom you are communicating understands you as you would like to be understood. In those times, when you are not interpreted correctly, you must rely on the hope that, in the final analysis, you will be given the benefit of the doubt. There are times when you will never know.

In their book, *The Blended Family,* authors Adrienne and Tom Frydenger stress how our tone and body are "giveaways" for our real feelings. Little wonder, then, that parents become upset with children who definitely are not listening to the "words." Long before the lecture begins, children have already received the essence of the message by the manner in which their parents bring it to them. Pointed fingers, raised voices, angry eyes, all betray what is really being communicated: the anger and disappointment felt by the adult. Details are irrelevant to a child who knows he has let his parents down.

As adults when we try to mask our tone, negative feelings often come across in body language. Very few people are really fooled. The body can show many emotions, including tension, and does so involuntarily. Better perhaps to come out with our feelings in the first place. My friend Ilona has a wonderful saying regarding communicating our feelings honestly: *Spit it out and kick sand over it!* Communicating our true feelings and leaving them behind with the "kitty litter" may sound admirable, but is not accomplished as easily by some of us as by others.

One last word about communicating honestly. *Belated honesty* is much more serious than missing a birthday by a few days. If honesty is left for too long a period, it can be damaging to relationships, as well as being difficult to recover from. I am not writing of the feelings we mask for short periods and later confess to another, but of the kind of hurt that can come from long periods of unexpressed feelings, leading to the accumulation of many small transgressions and possible gross misinterpretations in the meantime. There comes a point of no return when we finally spit out our honest feelings and they come across with such intensity that neither person in the relationship can easily get past them. The core of the relationship may have been damaged. In my experience, it is usually the one who has the most to atone for, and thus feels the most guilt, who cannot get past the heart-to-heart. The old adage, *We must learn to forgive ourselves first*, applies here. Business partnerships, as well as marriages and close friendships, are all vulnerable to belated honesty which can potentially cause their ultimate demise. It has happened to me.

Disguising Fights

Dr. Lee Salk is a firm advocate of expressing honest feelings when there is disharmony in the household. Salk has observed that parents are often guilty of disguising fights in the hope that this will protect the child. Quite the opposite, it will only increase a child's anxiety. Although Dr. Salk does not specifically extend his advice to blended families, I believe that he would apply the same standard of honest communication. My own experience backs this up.

Over the years, I was never quite sure whether Elizabeth and Robert should be allowed to witness the exchange of angry words between David and myself. But one can only keep the pretense of total harmony going for so long before the anger expresses itself in other ways. Children are far too sensitive not to feel the bad vibrations and leaving the cause to their imaginations is a far more destructive alternative than giving them an explanation. The degree to which honesty is expressed is a personal matter which you must come to terms with individually and as a couple.

In the past, my reluctance to honestly admit David and I, too, had our problems was very much related to our family pipeline and to my sense of false pride. God forbid if Heather should get wind of our difficulties I thought! Many couples feel this way, I'm sure. It is difficult to admit that our marriages are less than ideal, more so to have our ex-mate hear about it. The fact remains that generally the ability to openly admit our difficulties to our children is better than pussy-footing around the truth. I temper this by cautioning that common-sense judgment in what our children are able to handle should be exercised. However, if truths are buffered by humor, it is amazing what children are able to understand. It can do much to salvage a bad day.

Inappropriate Fears: Opening Up And Pulling Back

On the other hand, it is a very nice feeling to stay up late with one's stepchildren and really talk around the kitchen table. As Elizabeth and Robert approached their preteen years, I found that frequent open discussion facilitated the growth of a new kind of friendship between us.

Before this was possible, however, I had to first accept them as young individuals who were indeed growing up. I resisted, even feared, this for a time, as many adults do.

When Robert arrived with a "rat tail," and Elizabeth first appeared at the breakfast table wearing turquoise eye shadow, I thought, how bizarre! In typical stepmother fashion, I vowed that Adam and Annie would not be given my permission for this at such a young age. Robert picked up on my reaction and amused himself further by telling me the rat tail had been his mother's idea. To my horror, Adam wanted to grow one right away. And in time, he did.

Elizabeth soon realized that raking leaves with turquoise eye shadow seemed like a lot of bother, and the novelty wore thin (at our house anyway). Robert, too, had tired of the tail and was simply not cutting his hair at all. Meanwhile, I was mellowing in my attitudes, having reminded myself that my own parents had forced me to wash my face, almost daily, before catching the school bus, and for what? So that I could re-apply the makeup in the girls' washroom at school.

As Elizabeth and Robert became older, I let myself express my opinions more freely. At the same time, I felt somewhat inhibited because of Heather. I worried that if I was too open with her children, she would react with anger, thinking I was overstepping my role. This is largely because I have always felt a special empathy for pre-adolescence, a time which I remember vividly. Preteen worries, secret desires, confusing bodily changes, and the drama of day-to-day relationships at school are things which I find easy to talk about. If I opened up completely, perhaps my stepchildren would respond. And I wondered how Heather might react. My memory of the feelings I came to have for a special aunt and my best friend's mother had me thinking twice. At the time, these women always seemed more understanding than my own mother. I was at a very impressionable and critical age, and understand now that my mother was often hurt because I did not entrust her with all my anxieties. I did not wish to recreate the same situation between Heather and me.

It was a situation I had experienced in the past when I discovered that my girlfriend's children were comparing me to their mother. When Lea and I met, she was a new

single parent, and her family was hurting from the adjustment. Jenny and Tim felt their mother was sad and too
serious much of the time. Feeling burdened with financial
and career worries, I could understand this. As well, Lea
felt it was important to discipline her kids considering
how vulnerable they were to peer influence at ages eleven
and twelve.

Suddenly, I appeared in their lives on weekends: un-
married, childless and full of humor. While their mother
had been rationing her paycheck to provide the basics
(half of their fashion and toy wants were already out of
the question), Angie breezed in with grocery bags of junk
foods for the evening. "Every family needs an evening
now and again, with a good dose of junk, don't you agree?"
I said, with Jenny and Tim jumping around me in delight.
"Gee, Mom, you never do this — *see*, Angie thinks junk
food is okay!" they said reproachfully to their mother. My
friend handled it cheerfully because she knew I meant
well, but in my own way I had innocently come between
her and her children. The more open, spontaneous, liberated and generous I seemed, the more Jenny and Tim
compared. No mother can win when children have become
"little judges."

As always, the axiom, *What goes around comes around*, applies sooner or later. It took a number of years, but I came
to experience first-hand what Lea felt as a mother, when
my five-year-old, Annie, became infatuated with my
friend and neighbor, Hope, across the street. What was so
much better about Hope than me, I wondered? Annie
knew. It was the way Hope took extra time to cuddle her
and ask Annie questions; my friend played with her in the
pool like a little kid and bought my daughter a little heart
brooch with "Annie" engraved on it. Shortly after Annie's
first sleep-over with Gordie, Hope's preschooler, my
daughter confided that she wished she could live at Hope's
house and come visit me because Hope was her best
friend. I was absolutely shattered.

A year later Annie was similarly impressed with my
new friend, Carrie, who loved children and, having none

of her own, really enjoyed playing with my daughter. As she piggy-backed up and down the street with Annie, I was happy for them both, inwardly pleased with myself for having matured enough to realize that every child sees something wonderful in one of Mom's special friends.

When Carrie invited us to Toronto Island along with another girlfriend and her six-year-old stepdaughter, she now had two little ones to go on rides with. I had taken along Adam and was relieved that Carrie was keeping my two from fighting. It was interesting, however, to witness how over the course of the afternoon, Carrie's friend was becoming increasingly annoyed at the way her stepdaughter was clinging to Carrie. When we stepped off the ferry boat, and the little girl clung to Carrie and would not come when called, I watched her stepmother pull her possessively to her side and whisper for her to "Stay put, once and for all." The child began to cry, but stayed put. Sad as it made me feel for the both of them, I also understood. Her stepmother had reacted childishly, feeling somehow that after all of her time and energy, she rated "second" in popularity. The reality was, on that day, she had. In the eyes of a child, mothers and stepmothers do at times. Then again, there are moments when they are told they're the best!

Last winter I volunteered to be a driver on my son's school trip to the local art center. Every little girl in the class had great fun burying herself in my massive beaver coat. One young girl, who seemed especially taken with my antics, blurted out, "I wish you were my mother!"

"Not if you lived with me," I answered. "Ask Adam!"

And there lies the crux: I have always been able to laugh and joke freely with children, especially teens, when I am spared the day-to-day responsibility of their development. That does not mean to imply that I'm not as much fun with my own children at times, but they get *all* of me. That means the mother who disciplines also worries, is distracted, tired and emotional.

With Elizabeth and Robert I very much wanted to share the experiences and feelings of my teen years with them.

And, because I was not their full-time stepmother, it was easier for me to empathize with them on issues they were facing. I knew that I sometimes appeared very open and easy going. My fear was that I would allow myself to compete with Heather and that was the last thing I wished. Possibly Heather would never have reacted negatively if Elizabeth and Robert had made the odd comparison in my favor, but I did not wish to risk it; she was after all *the ex* in my life. One evening, however, I let my guard down and had a wonderful time.

The mood had been good all day, and I felt especially talkative. Adam and Annie, as well as David, had gone to bed early. Elizabeth, Robert and I had lit a candle and were hunched over the kitchen table munching popcorn. I started things off by asking simply what they thought they might like to be when they got older. Neither of them was sure. Give me an audience, and I'll give you a story: I shared with them my life in a girls' dormitory at the university. They loved it.

Later I chastised myself for my openness. What was I doing I thought? Perhaps Heather would become angry with me over the things I was planting in their heads. I had just spent an hour encouraging them both to go to a university and get the best degree they could. Perhaps they would repeat the conversation and she would think it her place, not mine, to talk about education. Perhaps, perhaps . . .

That evening I had felt a special closeness toward Elizabeth and Robert in which they, too, were seeing me not as Dad's wife, or Adam and Annie's mother, but as Angie. My individuality had been able to shine. I had felt this same appreciation of me when Elizabeth and I promoted the third cookbook together at the book fair. For the first time, she saw me functioning in the business world as Angela, not as mother and stepmother, but as a working writer.

Having laid myself bare that evening, I later regressed to my former, safer role as the Angie who sometimes made great food and let Dad engineer many of the weekend activities. Unfortunately, Heather's angry outburst at David dove-tailed with this period, which made me evade intimate discussions with Elizabeth and Robert all the more.

Theodore Isaac Rubin, author of *One on One*, would have labeled my reaction an *inappropriate fear*. Heather had really given me no cause to worry in the past; it was my anticipation of her possible anger which caused me to back off from the children. And when she had vented her anger at David, I assumed I might be next. It never happened. For that misinterpretation, I paid a large price, the loss of closeness with Elizabeth and Robert for a long time. I had played "Simon Says" with their feelings: "Angie says: let's have a real heart-to-heart, and take five paces toward emotional intimacy." Three weeks later: "Angie says: take six paces back; let me be the way I was before."

I never had the nerve to admit my fears openly and disappointed myself by pulling back as I had done. Elizabeth and Robert did not understand my feelings toward Heather then, and I didn't feel it right to ask them not to repeat my personal stories to her. So I stopped telling stories. In retrospect, I over-analyzed the situation and assumed too much, thinking Heather would come to feel defensive if I influenced her children through our discussions. My feelings, however, were still my real feelings, and that in itself is all right. What was *not* all right was my inability to communicate why I wasn't comfortable with close discussions in the future. Out of respect for Elizabeth and Robert, that would have been a good thing for our relationship. By the time Angie next said, "Let's go five paces forward in emotional intimacy," Elizabeth and Robert had evolved into teenagers and weren't interested in me or that game any longer.

9

The Meaning Of Trust

The real voyage of discovery consists not in seeking new landscapes, but in having new eyes.

Marcel Proust

My father is a wonderful storyteller and can retell the classical myths in a way I have never been able to read. In reflecting on the nature of trust, the mythical figure Argus came to mind.

According to my father, the gods dwelled in splendid castles close to the Sun. There, they could observe the mortals from on high. Love affairs between the gods and mortal maidens were not uncommon, and of them all, Father Zeus was especially known for his philanderings. Zeus was aware that his wife Hera had become suspicious of him, and to cloak himself and his newest love Io, he slipped numerous clouds around his castle to obscure Hera's view, so that the earth appeared shrouded in darkness. Hera was no fool, however, and moved a cloud aside to watch her husband. Realizing suddenly that he and his maiden were under his wife's full gaze, Zeus quickly transformed Io into a beautiful snow white cow. The shrewd Hera pretended to be taken by the cow's beauty and asked Zeus to present it to her as a gift, which the god had no choice but to do. Having transformed his beloved into a cow, Zeus found himself trapped; Hera had placed her faithful hundred-eyed watchman, Argus, over poor Io as guard. Day and night, Argus kept watch over the white cow, never closing more than half of his one hundred eyes. Zeus was beside himself.

Apparently even in the earliest times, men were known to "stick together," my father told me. So Zeus called in the aid of his son, Hermes, who not only told wonderful tales, but played magically on the pan flute as well. Instructed by his father to kill the hundred-eyed Argus, Hermes disguised himself as a herdsman, then spoke and played so charmingly that Hera's servant soon became drowsy. At length, one eye after another began to close until, at last, Hermes had lulled all one hundred eyes to sleep. He sprang up and cut off Argus' head with one swift blow of his sword. Zeus quickly returned Io into her original maiden form. Hera was grief-stricken over the loss of her faithful Argus and placed his hundred eyes into the tail of her own bird, the Peacock.

A delightful myth, but aside from the obvious, what has Argus to do with the nature of trust, you ask?

In my mind, Argus has come to symbolize the non-trusting, those who are by nature "watchful," those who have a hundred inner eyes which never close completely, unless by chance they are enchanted into sleep. If you are an Argus, you are slow and unwilling to trust. And when you finally do, your worst suspicions are confirmed; you lose your head! You feel betrayed. Non-trust (Argus), then, is the faithful servant of fear (Hera). Look for betrayal, watch for it day and night as Argus did, and it will come, as sure as any self-fulfilling prophecy. The fact that Zeus deserved the mistrust is less the point for me in the myth than Hera, who spent her waking energy looking to confirm it. In the end, she had neither Zeus' fidelity nor her faithful Argus.

I present the tale not to advise that we should all be a sleeping Argus, but rather to say that honesty and trust go hand in hand. Fear is the enemy of that trust.

In a blended family, it may appear sometimes that the world is the hundred-eyed Argus watching *you*. To find your own level of balanced trust, however, the task is not to look to the hundred eyes within yourself nor the hundred eyes without, but rather to practice the laying aside of pretense and discover the art of real openness. This is a form of trust in which you simply say, "This is me, as I really feel and am. Accept my vulnerabilities and allow me also to accept yours." How many of us really say this in our relationships?

Letting Go Of Pretense

Unfortunately in a blended family, there are ofen too many things to prove. Ex-spouses may still be trying to show one another in spoken or unspoken terms, "Look at me, I'm fine without you. I don't need you at all." And what second wife or stepmother allows herself to expose her vulnerabilities to her husband's ex-wife, her stepchildren, or even to the man she loves? At the root lies fear — inappropriate or otherwise.

In examining myself, I acknowledge that, in some ways, I have been more open than many second wives, yet it has taken me many years to arrive at a point where I now feel comfortable exposing my vulnerabilities. While writing my third cookbook in which my stepchildren participated and appeared on the cover, I was still trying to maintain an image of cohesive togetherness. I focused only on the "ups" and rarely acknowledged the "downs" to anyone outside of close family. When Elizabeth and I attended a Booksellers Convention together with sample recipes, I was highly offended by a woman's passing remark: "How diplomatic of you to include your stepchildren on the cover!" Our family life was good, I thought to myself. Why wouldn't I include Elizabeth and Robert?

True as that was, how could I not if I wished to maintain that closeness? When my publisher suggested we use Adam and Annie, plus two other children with a multicultural appearance, I couldn't conceive of agreeing, in consideration for Elizabeth's and Robert's feelings. In a small way, perhaps, it had been a diplomatic decision and was my way of showing them visibly that I valued their involvement in my life.

Before I was able to let go of pretense, I, too, had "Argus eyes" and lived with my share of fears. Many of my actions were motivated by needless worry about what might happen, or how events might be interpreted. On the whole my inappropriate fears had their genesis in my desire to live up to an image I had created for myself. Other fears developed as I internalized expectations which I allowed my family to place upon me.

Talking myself into feeling intimidated by Paul's former wife Linda is an example of how I chose to create a "score card" of her attributes versus mine. This game had only one player — me. And I always lost. In order to lose, my *outer Argus* dwelled on her beauty, fine career, and all I could *see*. Each time Paul told me that he had stopped regarding Linda as good-looking long ago, my *inner Argus* remembered the description he had given me of his impressions when he first noticed her sitting with two girlfriends in the campus cafeteria. "I knew instantly this was the girl I would marry," he had told me. A little too honest for a new companion to hear, don't you think?

I'm certainly not the first who found an ex-wife's beauty difficult to ignore, and not the first who took some time to believe her lover's reassurances. The key, as I see it now, was my lack of self-trust, in my own outer as well as inner beauty.

Envy And Jealousy

Consider another example, also relevant to many women: my friend Lydia, who really doesn't look fat, but is unhappy with her weight. She turns to her husband time and time again for reassurance. This man can talk until "the cows come home," and he will never convince her on that essential inner level, that she is indeed not unattractively fat. This could just as well be an issue over her nose size, small breast, size ten shoe, or any other physical feature she feels negative about. Her insecurities will not allow her to believe that which she would most desire. The very feature she lacks may make her envious and jealous of others.

In his book *Compassion and Self-Hate*, Theodore Rubin makes the distinction between envy and jealousy in this way. Those who envy feel that they are deprived of the very thing which all others have much more of; those who are jealous feel that in comparison to others, who have much to give, they have little if anything to give. My understanding of this is that envy is seen in terms of concrete, enviable things, jealousy in terms of intangible feelings of scarcity. Thus the emotion of envy makes you feel depleted in your ability to *have;* jealousy makes you feel depleted in your ability to *give.* Both emotions are destructive to your Self as well as to your relationships and require a good deal of self-scrutiny and understanding to overcome.

The semantics of the words "envy" and "jealousy" are less important, I feel, than their negative impact. Our attachment to *things* makes us vulnerable to these emotions. Our tendency to look to others whom we admire does as well.

In a society which feeds our addiction for all things material, what of those couples who have accumulated personal possessions and mementos together? Divide and conquer is the name of the game at separation. There are couples whose personal attitudes to money and possessions are so complex that by the time they divorce, what began as a civilized break, ends in petty haggling over who is entitled to which wedding gift. Whatever is materially gained in such disputes only remains behind as reminders of *things* once shared with another partner. After a bitter separation, it is a small consolation; too many mementos may even serve to irritate by their presence alone.

Both David and I had put very little emphasis on personal belongings when we left our former relationships. Paul's very real concern, however, was that he would be stripped twice. I knew how he had felt about losing the antique spool bed, as well as other things Linda had taken from the house. They had fussed their way through detailed lists, using the other's favorite pieces as levers for negotiation. When I expressed my wish for half of the English Blue Chelsea china of which I was especially fond, he refused, reasoning that the original starter pieces had come with his house, and he did not now wish to divide the 12-service set. Not wanting to niggle, I withdrew myself emotionally from all things shared in the house. I essentially left with a number of kitchen basics and moved into a furnished apartment. My parents, horrified by my foolishness, found it inconceivable that, after five years of working at a respectable job, I had less materially than when Paul and I had first met.

I did not bemoan my choices and felt strongly that for me, in the long run, it was best. From a practical standpoint, it certainly appeared as if I were in a "deficit position." That was true, but much more on an inner level; nothing I could have taken with me would have made me feel less depleted. The *stripping*, as such, happens emotionally long before you physically separate.

The positive aspect, however, was that it allowed me the new beginnings I was looking for; and in a real sense, because David was in the same position, it gave us both the chance to start "from scratch."

That is not to say, however, that I would recommend this "exit" for everyone; it was merely "my style" and somehow suited me in many ways at the time. Without children to think about and as a working young woman, I was in a good position to break away in this manner. I did not envy the next Mrs. Paul who would move into his home with the material traces of two women around her. It had taken me long enough to feel that indeed his home was now also mine. Buying a new bed, which Paul did, was no doubt symbolic of his need to put our relationshp behind him; renovating the kitchen also did much to help his new companion feel they were sharing a house which included her personal imprint.

For other couples who have amassed goods together, I do not believe it is necessary to part with everything they hold dear. A mature attitude, as well as trust, should make it possible to accept a new spouse who has retained things which remind both of you of a former partner. Of the few items which David brought into our marriage, he still cherishes the gun cabinet, a gift from Heather years ago. If one can get past the hurts and incompatibilities, such things can come to represent symbolic tokens of what was once good between you. If a divorced couple has children, it is a very nice thing for them to know and see that Dad or Mom still value that which they acquired and shared while still together.

The ability to do this, as well as to accept the presence of past mementos associated with your husband's ex-wife, varies from person to person. A friend of mine (also a second wife) seemed to have no trouble dealing with a large oil portrait of her husband's deceased wife. It continually astounded her friends to see it hanging in the dining room.

The Willingness To Trust

Once again self-trust and the trust extended to one's partner make the crucial difference. Without a sense of self-esteem, real openness and trust are not possible. It would be naive, however, to think that *instant trust* is attainable in stepfamilies. The building of trust requires repeated efforts as well as frequently giving the benefit of the doubt. First of all you must want to trust, for as willing as you may be, the test of time will inevitably also test that trust. And as your relationship is being tested, feelings of trust toward your mate will either be cemented or broken.

If your partner has consistently merited your trust, strong bonds are built between you which act as a basis for giving the benefit of the doubt at some future time when your relationship is challenged again. The best relationship is one which has progressed to the point where a trusting action by one creates a trusting reaction in the other. If this is the case, giving the benefit of the doubt will seem like little effort.

This issue really concerns our very nature, whether we are essentially trusting or non-trusting to begin with. Those who are *not*, can be married to someone who gives no grounds for mistrust for years and yet, for them the slightest evidence of doubt will cause a wave of mistrust to wash over the marriage. This is extremely difficult for the one deserving of the trust to take. If that person feels unjustly mistrusted long enough, it will eventually poison the relationship to the degree where this spouse may well act out in the manner which was first suspected. Just as love requires your time and effort to keep it alive, so also does trust. In your desire to view the world and others through optimistic eyes, you must consciously also decide to put fear aside and become a more trusting individual.

It has been shown to me time and time again that if I demonstrate a willingness to believe in another person first, more often than not that person completely lives up to my expectations. My parents have, on occasion, chastised me for expecting only good motives of others. Their feelings about this are purely protective as they have also seen me feel disappointed and betrayed.

On these occasions I reacted by retreating within myself for a period. Openness then was lost, and I experienced fears of what might happen if I trusted again. With the passage of time and its ability to heal, I found myself wanting again to give the world and others the benefit of the doubt. Barry Manilow has crooned it often when he sings, *"I'm ready to take a chance again . . ."* In the same song Manilow also acknowledges the price one must be willling to pay with the decision to trust again: "You get what you get when you go for it!" The risk is there, but so also is the potential reward.

At the beginning of my relationship with Heather, I was often queried about my feelings toward her. Whenever Heather was kind, I was asked, "How can you trust her?" The truth is that I didn't completely. But I wanted to. I also knew that David trusted her motives. Relying on my trust in his judgment, I chose to give Heather the benefit of the doubt. The few exceptions which I described in earlier chapters were the only times that I did not feel easy in my trust toward her. I consider myself fortunate to have been the recipient of her trust as well; had it been otherwise, we would have likely exchanged angry words by now.

Trusting And Non-Trusting Partners

How does a basically trusting person relate to one who cannot bring himself to trust others? Unfortunately not as openly as one would like to. Within a family, each of us knows someone who is suspicious by nature. This person will be secretive about his financial affairs as well as his feelings. Afraid of betrayal or to appear the naive fool, he cannot take the risk of trusting. The reason often is that the very negative motives this person attributes to others are often ones he himself is guilty of in his dealings with people. In other words, he sees the world reflected in his own mirror. Given the very fact that his *own* thoughts and deeds are not always honorable, how then can he conceive that others will deal with him in ways which are always kind, generous and loving? This individual is surprised and unbelieving when he sees someone do good without expectation of payment. He believes that everything has its strings attached, everything must be repaid and accounted for. With family and friends, as with business, he will throughout his life carry with him a score card in which trust is no measuring factor.

If you find yourself in a relationship with someone who cannot trust, the best defense is to not take this mistrust personally. Know instead that, were it not for you, the world would indeed mirror the negativity which such a person expects. Know also that the reason mistrustful people seek out "Pollyannas" is because on a deep level, they very much yearn to trust and are possibly even jealous of your ability to do so. If possible, it is best to accept the reality that you will never be understood completely as you would like and may often be judged the "dreamer" or the "idealist," when in fact you see yourself as perfectly realistic. Rather, bolster yourself with Walt Whitman's words: *Faith is the antiseptic of the soul.*

Despite these inspiring words, non-trusting individuals are very much a part of any blended family. Some second wives are compelled to believe that their husband's former wife is "out to get every penny she can lay her hands on." Then again, some husbands run in circles to cleverly manipulate their equity so as not to be "taken to the cleaners." The fact that these phrases have such a familiar ring to our ears attest to their reality among divorcing men and women. A point made earlier comes to mind: Does a mistrustful second wife think the ex is out for every penny because that is exactly what she would be doing if placed in the same situation? Through what mirror is she seeing her world? And will her fears subside if she sees no indication of this happening? The answer lies in the deep roots of her nature established when she was still a child. If her viewpoint is non-trusting, changing now will be a difficult undertaking, although it is possible if she is genuinely committed to do so.

I believe that learning to give the benefit of the doubt is torturous for those who have difficulty with trust. So, too, is learning to really love; for love also requires trust. When non-trusting individuals allow themselves to really love, they find themselves waffling between wanting to trust and not wholly being able to, creating destructive cycles of positive and negative feelings.

A love relationship between trusting and non-trusting individuals requires many demonstrations of unconditional love from the trusting spouse, as well as open and honest communication whenever situations arise that have tested the other partner's ability to trust. However, even unconditional love has its limits. Blind faith and unconditional love can only go so far before the partner doing all the trusting possibly finds himself with the same affliction. I have seen beautiful trusting individuals turn sour on others through the long-term influence of a non-trusting partner.

As for my relationship with Heather, although my ability to trust in many areas developed gradually, we did, however, from the onset have one unspoken trust between us — we would *never* belittle or discredit the other to the children. Within the blended family, that basic trust is essential to the growth of all other areas of trust.

Another area in which I came to trust Heather was in her ability to be sensitive to family situations when the appearance of a man's ex-wife together with his current wife would create an awkward atmosphere. A family funeral is a perfect example. Tune in to any soap opera and you would almost be inclined to believe otherwise. These characters thrive on their emotional tennis matches with one another; positive feelings such as trust don't make for good drama.

I, for one, admit to more conventional attitudes when put to the test in potentially tense situations. Fortunately for me, Heather was sensitive to this.

When David's father died, it created an awkward situation in our family. Heather, as former daughter-in-law, would also have liked to pay her respects at the funeral. I was most uncomfortable when I visualized the scene in which both of us would attend the funeral and family gatherings afterwards. Anticipating this, Heather called David's mother to express her sympathy and advised us she would not be attending.

My friend who owns a funeral home tells me that this is the norm. Former wives often pay their respects to the deceased at the funeral home before the service. According to the owner, most second wives feel ill at ease during this time and react in much the same way I did. Whether Heather wished to attend or whether she thought Eliza-

beth and Robert were too young to experience a funeral,
the fact remains that she had the choice to go and did not.
This sensitive issue is one that must, after all, be left to
each individual. Ultimately, each of us must decide what
feels comfortable. And as the children grow, they, too,
have their choices.

Bonding And Shared History

Trust facilitates bonding in relationships. There are
many kinds of wonderful bonds that grow between people
and which vary in intensity. Bonds of affection and respect can be very satisfying. A bond of friendship can
grow and become just as powerful as a bond of love. The
parent/child bond is very important to both the adult and
child and cannot be duplicated by the stepparent.

To duplicate David's relationship with his children was
not my goal; what I did want, however, was to create a
close-knit stepfamily circle in which I could relate to Elizabeth and Robert as well as I related to Adam and Annie.
What I needed to learn, however, was that I could love
David's children *differently* from my own and still not take
away from the love they shared with their mother or father, or the love I shared with Annie and Adam. For me, it
was not so much a question of competition, as the realiza-
tion that children have more than enough varied levels of
love to spread around. An emotionally healthy parent or
stepparent should also have enough love to allow children
to express their feelings of affection or love to others.

It is the wise stepparent who does not analyze the nature of the love or positive feelings a child has for someone
else. It is an "emotional set-up" for competition.

As I see it now, each close relationship you have creates
its own special history. You bring the newness of your
talents, experiences, heritage, interests and much more to
another human being. And you gain something from the
other which you may not have experienced in any other
friendship, each with its own shared history. Thus, when
Elizabeth watches *Coronation Street* and speaks fondly of

her Nan, I see that they have developed a special history based on a grandparent/child love. Times that Elizabeth and Robert shared with us gave them a history of Saturday bike rides, fried egg sandwiches, and mattresses dragged from the basement, among other memories.

Within your blended family circle, in order to best achieve a sense of family as well as your own unique shared history, you must first offer your *real self*, that is, to be willing to give. In doing so, you will certainly make mistakes and likely misinterpret others and be misinterpreted. Time, energy and love, consistently shared, will contribute to feelings of security which give you that sense of family togetherness you're aiming for. As I see it, there is no need for any set of relationships in which Elizabeth and Robert have to interfere or compete with one another. Each establishes its own level of trust, has its own shared history, and bonds in its own way.

If one person sets up barriers, no bond can be developed or sustained. If a child sets up barriers with his own parents, although the mutual bond may be broken for a time, the parent will still feel the bond with his heart. The writers of *Lifeprints* confirm by their research that a parent at some point automatically bonds with his child, and this parent/child bond will likely last a lifetime. When Elizabeth and Robert temporarily distanced themselves from our household as they reached their teen years, David felt the parent/child bond with them no less; neither did I lose or wish to deny the bond I had established with them. Similarly, David and I chose to trust the feeling that his children, though outwardly disinterested, nevertheless retained their emotional ties with us.

As with all things, bonding included, one must strive for a healthy balance. It is considered excessive, in terms of bonding, when a parent considers a child so much a part of themselves that whatever the child does will either be to that parent's credit or shame. The child is not viewed then as an individual, but rather as an extension of the parent's image. There is far too much emphasis placed then on the achievements and failures of the child, precisely because they are seen as the parent's achievements or failures. This is bonding taken to the extreme. The fact is that many of us have felt these very pressures in our childhood.

To some degree most parents find themselves doing this occasionally. When my children do something terrific to make me feel proud, I naturally feel inclined to think that, in part, it has been through my influence on them. Conversely if one of the children displays a lack of social skills at preschool, it is my nature to question myself whether I have failed and what I could do to correct the behavior. When Adam experienced extreme shyness at nursery school, his teacher, whose approach I admired, reassured me by explaining that his introversion was "just Adam," which he might or might not outgrow. She had accepted his individuality long before I had. Sometimes the parent/child bond places the parent in too close a position for proper objectivity. I struggle always to maintain a balance.

The absence of this parent/child bond is the very reason that a stepmother has the potential to become a good friend to her husband's children. She does not have the emotional investment in the children to quite the same degree that the biological parent has. If trust is present and circumstances allow it, the stepmother can see parent/child disputes more objectively and possibly act as mediator, (although she takes the risk of having both parties become angry with her). In some stepfamilies, a second wife may even be able to offer sisterly advice to an adolescent girl; however, I would think that this would be a good idea only if the stepdaughter does not put her stepmother in a compromising position. It might be wise to query the girl on her mother's wishes first, before giving out contradictory advice.

To be approached by one's stepchild for advice would mean that a great deal of trust had been established within your relationship, and this takes time. Studies show that the relationship between a child and stepmother develops very, very slowly. In the early years of a remarriage, many children feel very little attachment to their stepmothers. Findings indicate that younger children are much more likely to develop warm and close relationships with their stepmothers. I believe this relates to the inherent trusting nature in most young children.

These observations have certainly verified themselves in my blended family. When I met Elizabeth and Robert, as three- and four-year-old children, they were spontaneously verbal and cuddly. I had very little to do to win them over. They lived much more in the moment of play and were less concerned about structured family activities. David and I had little concern for their boredom. As they grew older and more self-conscious, I experienced moments of shyness from them when they arrived Friday evenings. In contrast to their younger years, Elizabeth and Robert went through a phase when, between the ages of nine through 12, they re-established their attachment to me. Our bonding was a gradual process, with periods of greater and lesser attachment and corresponding levels of trust.

In order to understand step-bonding and trust fully and honestly, it is important to acknowledge the possible feelings of favoritism and ambivalence a stepmother may feel toward one or more of her husband's children. It becomes a sensitive issue in "regular" nuclear families as well, and parents are reluctant to face their own feelings on this issue. When you hear a mother refer to "her problem child," you can be sure that she also has ambivalent feelings toward that child. My friend, Debbie, admitted to this freely. She had always enjoyed a close relationship with her daughter, but found herself in regular battles of will with her son. In her words, "It was much easier to love the little girl." She used to feel guilty about this and bent herself backwards to show patience toward the boy. Since facing her ambivalence, she has become more honest with him and their relationship has relaxed considerably.

Just as the teacher has a "pet," the aunt a favorite niece, it is too human after all to feel especially drawn to one personality more than another. The children's ages, temperaments, or just that one seems to be a "kindred spirit" who reacts positively to the stepparent, are all factors which affect us. Very little can be done except to make an effort to be equal in other areas. One word of advice regarding young children: although they may sense emotional biases, never show favoritism through goods bought. Little children are very aware of who receives what. This is brought to my attention every time I go shopping with only one child and unthinkingly fail to bring a treat for the child waiting at home. Unforgivable!

To the world or outside family observer, our blended family may appear to be strange and rather artificial. There will always be people who continue to observe us with curiosity. It is difficult for them to imagine us harmoniously sharing our weekends and then continuing on with our separate households. What all blended families share was best illustrated for me by a small drawing in one of my research sources. The diagram showed two circles converging and overlapping. The portion common to both circles is the blended family life we share on weekends. Each circle is a separate household which represents most of our day-to-day lives, but the overlapping portion and the trust which is established within those times together is equally important. We cannot be holistically happy unless this small but crucial area also has harmony.

To summarize: Trust means that there is no price tag on our relationships, no sense of expecting something in return for every demonstration of loyalty on our part. Theodore Rubin, who has written extensively on trust in his book *One on One*, feels that people with a high level of trust are not concerned with getting their "fair share"; they know (and trust) that whatever they need will come to them. There is no sense of being "used" by others.

To trust that your partner will not use you makes pretense unnecessary and allows for honest communication and a truly open relationship. You can give each other the gift of freedom — to express exactly who you are, and what you think and feel, not that which you think your partner might wish to hear. David gave me this freedom from the beginning. Thus, I have always been able to tell him exactly what I thought of his family, his children, and our weekends together. Our degree of intimacy has grown in relation to the degree of openness we have been capable of.

Trust Is A Choice

Having established emotional intimacy in our marriage, the biggest challenge that David and I have always had is to consistently maintain that intimacy. Day-to-day worries and distractions can so easily intrude on a relationship and block communication. As a stepmother, I must always try to be in touch with my own feelings. Positive or negative, they need to be expressed to David if we are to remain open with one another. It does, however, all begin with a conscious decision to trust.

You may well ask, "Where do I start?"

Assuming that your husband has not blatantly betrayed you in the past, you begin by first *choosing* to trust your spouse. You must first decide that you want to trust him and that he deserves your trust and is worthy of it. In learning to trust, you must also come to terms with the degree of intimacy you wish to have, the kind of openness you need. Then ask yourself, "Is this the kind of intimacy my husband wishes or is capable of giving? Is he willing to be as open as I?" Once you have decided what degree of openness you need in your relationship, you can then acknowledge whether your partner is able to reciprocate. If his needs are different than yours, you have a choice: either try to change him or accept what he is able to give and trust that he loves you in his way.

Affirmations For Building Trust In Your Husband

In choosing to trust your husband, begin by affirming the following to yourself often:

1. I trust that he backs up my status with the children.
2. I trust that he allows me authority with his children should I wish to use it.

3. I trust that my needs are as important to him as his children's.
4. I trust that he includes me in his thoughts and plans regarding his children.
5. I trust that he protects my privacy as much as possible during discussions between himself and his ex-wife.
6. I trust that he is not secretive about money or financial matters pertaining to his children and ex-wife.
7. I trust that if he should have difficulties with his ex-wife, he would not take his frustration out on me.
8. I trust that he demonstrates respect and affection toward me in front of his children.

Just as I chose to trust David, you can decide to trust and learn, too, that it is possible to give trust *before* expecting it in return. This is the best way to begin a new pattern of relating to each other. Suspicion breeds mistrust. Now you have the opportunity to develop trust, first within yourself, beginning a new pattern which will encourage openness in your partner. In trusting, you open the door to a more comfortable atmosphere. Tensions ease and defenses can be lowered.

Affirmations For Closer Family Relationships

When you are inclined not to trust, you will initially have difficulty giving the benefit of the doubt, and it may feel like a lot of effort to do so. Help yourself to trust by talking to yourself often. Your inner dialogue can say many positive things, all of which affirm your desire to trust. Tell yourself:

1. I now have a close relationship.
2. I believe that I am loved, that I am important to him.
3. I want to help create a strong family unit. If all of us learn to trust more, we will become stronger.
4. Children learn by example. If my stepchildren see that I am trusting, they will trust more.
5. I demonstrate my trust by being more open with him. I express my true feelings and encourage the same in him.

6. I do not become defensive when he tells me his true feelings.

7. In learning to trust, I have stopped imagining the negative, as well as trying to second guess or drawing my own conclusions.

Affirmations For Building Trust With Your Stepchildren

Once you are able to feel trust and openness toward your husband, you must decide whether you are able to give trust to his children. Once again, in making the effort, some inner dialogue may be necessary during times when otherwise you might feel anxious, threatened, jealous or alone. Trusting older children may be more difficult than trusting younger children. Each age group requires a different sort of trust and understanding from you. With stepchildren, your inner dialogue can tell you this:

1. If they seem to be ignoring me, it is because they are comfortable in my home and don't feel the pressure of being on their best behavior.

2. They probably ignore their mother: Why should it be otherwise, if they are relaxed?

3. It is natural for all children to have certain food preferences. They are not trying to insult me; they simply don't like that food, dish, etc.

4. It is natural for children to wish to cuddle with their dad. They have a mother to cuddle full-time.

5. Children don't enjoy chores. I shouldn't expect them to offer. They must be reminded at home to help, too.

6. When they badger for things or goodies on shopping trips, they are not trying to manipulate their father to spend more money on them. It is natural for children to want more.

7. They are not talking about their mother deliberately to upset me. Young children always chatter about people who matter to them.

8. Teens often seek variety and action. If my stepchildren appear bored, it is not a reflection of how they feel about me.

9. Young people often withdraw to be quiet and alone. It's an age of mood swings. There's nothing I've done to cause it.

10. Just because my stepdaughter is staring at me doesn't mean she is comparing me to her mother or wondering what her father saw in me.

11. It is natural for young girls to become diet conscious. She is not using her diet as an excuse to reject my food. She probably does the same thing at home.

12. When my stepchildren comment on something new that I or their stepsiblings have acquired, they do not have a mental score card tabulating what *we* have versus what *they* have.

13. My stepson is always picking things I don't like to do, but that does not mean he's trying to exclude me to be alone with his dad. I just haven't discovered what we all like to do yet.

14. Boys sometimes feel shy talking to women. My stepson is not trying to direct his conversation to his father to offend me. I must give him time to feel comfortable.

If you feel that you can be open and more trusting toward your husband and his children, try to apply the same positive attitude toward family members on your husband's side. If you are inclined to react negatively, it is possible to imagine any number of comparisons your in-laws may be making between you and their former daughter-in-law. Even if you have been given reason to mistrust, try to block out the negative with inner dialogue. Attributing negative motives to these people will only harm you in the end. Do you really want to believe that your mother-in-law thinks Betty's pies are better than yours, or that she wished you would stay home to raise the children as Lorna did? Not likely. Learn to give the benefit of the doubt until these negatives are spoken to you directly.

Affirmations For Building Trust With His Ex

Giving trust to your husband's former wife may be the most difficult of all. In learning to be more positive, your inner dialogue can tell you this:

1. My husband's ex-wife does not send the kids so poorly dressed to show us how badly off she is. Perhaps she's behind in laundry or believes weekends are for "play clothes."
2. My husband's ex-wife visits with his mother so that the children can keep in touch with their grandparents and because she probably enjoys his parents' company. She is not going to gossip about me.
3. The children are not aloof because their mother is trying to poison them against me.
4. When my husband's ex-wife calls him at work, there is a good reason for it. She is not playing coy.
5. Questions my stepchildren ask us do not mean their mother is pumping them for information.
6. It is just as difficult to be an ex-wife as it is to be a stepmother.

Learning To Write Your Own Affirmations

Now it is your turn. Take a separate sheet of paper and write your own personal concerns in a positive way. It is important that you write in the present tense as if the wished-for outcome is already a reality.

Self-defeating thoughts can be combated through positive inner dialogue. Someone in your family will think you a fool for choosing to think good instead of bad. Expect this, for if you think about it, those who will consider you naive, good-natured or too trusting are people who are not able to give trust easily themselves. They are likely in need of the same benefit of the doubt you are now willing to give your blended family. Someone has to start with a positive attitude, and it may as well be you.

10

Re-Commitment To Love

There is no remedy for love but to love more.
Henry David Thoreau

My relationship with David had its genesis in friendship, not infatuation. I shared with him, as a friend, an uncensored version of past experiences, hopes and dreams, from the perspective of one who had seen them crumble in her last relationship. Apparently, real honesty didn't disturb him and I felt surprisingly "safe." It would be easy to let myself love this man, I thought at the time.

That was the first conscious step I took in loving David. I clearly remember feeling awkward about considering whether I could, or should, love. When I telephoned my best friend, Tessie, I expressed my doubts: "This isn't the falling in love I've known. Where's the anxiety, the possessiveness, insecurity and sweaty palms?" David's love was giving me the leeway to move and express myself, as I really felt and was. Apparently, he had no interest in changing me, and I found myself not only liking, but loving him as well.

Author Scott Peck, who profoundly affected my thinking with his book *The Road Less Traveled*, has most clearly
defined for me the nature of "real love", love which I have
come to experience in my marriage with David. Peck sees
love as more *volitional* than *emotional* (although this does
not preclude our emotions). Real love is "effortful," writes
Peck, and involves our commitment to nurture the growth
of our partner's self, as well as our own. By consciously
giving attention to the other and by responding with loving deeds as well as thoughts, we demonstrate real love
which is self-enlarging as it makes room for the individuality and separateness of the person we love. This is
contrary to our former notions of a romantic, "two-
hearts-beating-as-one love," as well as myths associated
with the process of "falling in love."

The theme of love has always made good drama; unre-
quited love has kept classics alive. Minstrels long ago and
songwriters today still croon about the pain of love. The
romantic ideal of love, as we have always accepted it,
becomes a form of suffering. Psychoanalyst Carl Jung
once wrote: "Neurosis is always a substitute for legitimate
suffering." Is this not also partly true of love?

In contrast Scott Peck has an enlightened view of love.
He by-passes the intense *Sturm und Drang* aspect of loving
and focuses on the spiritual potential and freeing quality
that real love encourages in relationships. On the surface,
this may seem less intense; in reality, the growth of this
kind of love is very exciting.

Somewhere though, between *romantic love* and *real love*,
there is still a long road of effort. Whether you find yourself
within a mixed racial or inter-religious family, a blended
family, or are personally coping with a physical or emotional
handicap, human relationships are filled with complexities.
Life, fate or we ourselves bring about these circumstances.

The Cross-Road: Giving Up
Or Re-Committing

The passage of time invariably brings us to a cross-
road. Whether you have thrown yourself into a meaning-

ful relationship or have struggled with a personal inner commitment, you have perhaps become disenchanted, weary, or restless. You must come to a choice: To give up or to re-commit. If you choose to continue, it often requires a "second wind of love." And with this you will eventually experience growth and a deeper commitment.

The dark period that lies between the time of despair and confusion, and the time of renewed hope, is where we experience pain. Even the journey to Peck's "real love" cannot be made without some degree of suffering; and in that sense, love is indeed a legitimate form of suffering. The truth is that pain is often a pre-requisite to growth. Is it not the insights garnered from our negative experiences which give us the capacity for increased feelings of compassion for others? In re-committing then, we must learn to do as Thoreau suggests: "to love more," but in a self-enlarging way, for ourselves and those whom we love.

My holiday in Cococonk was one of my dark periods. I had gradually come to feel burdened by the "package deal" to which I had originally committed. My feelings had changed, and with those changes, I was compelled to reassess my needs. Whereas early in my marriage I had only looked for fulfillment through my family, I had arrived at a saturation point in patience and understanding. As I was chastising myself on the one hand, a large part of me yearned for more intellectual and creative stimulation and personal freedom. Other women were happy, why couldn't I be?

Although I didn't understand myself then, Theodore Rubin, psychologist and author of *Compassion and Self-Hate*, would have told me that I simply had two conflicting emotions on a parallel course, not an unusual anxiety for a complex human being. Gail Sheehy, social researcher and author of *Passages*, would have explained my distress as the transition from one *life passage* to another. My mother would have called it "just Angie."

However it was analyzed, it did cause me to rethink my attitudes. My priorities shifted; our lives took another direction, and I grew. We all did.

The basic question, however, still came to this: Did I want a loving "tight family" or not? Yes! And so I chose to work at developing my creative self together with maintaining a real effort for closeness with my stepfamily. I had come to a cross-road, but I also chose to re-commit to David, as well as to his children.

It is my belief that every second wife arrives at a similar crossroad. Leaving your stepfamily is not the issue; rather it is your willingness to continue working at achieving harmony within it. The only way this is possible is to demonstrate a positive, open and trusting attitude.

In your household where you do have some measure of control, don't sabotage the atmosphere by anticipating a slap in the face before you get one. And then if someone hurts you, by all means react, but also try to understand the motives behind their action. Tolerance, and the development of insight, require, above everything else, your ability to feel and demonstrate kindness.

Levels Of Caring

As a stepmother, you have three choices in relating to your blended family:

1. You can be cruel.
2. You can be indifferent.
3. You can be kind.

Cruelty is relative. A stepmother might consider herself cruel if she hoards treats for her children, not his. In my opinion that does not indicate cruelty, although it may be grounds for feeling guilty. Mental or physical cruelty, however, is a serious thing and any anxiety over this might be a sign that getting counseling is in order. If you feel yourself wanting to be nasty, either subtly or overtly, it's time to talk to someone. Family services have sympathetic counselors on hand, as well as an increasing variety of step-parenting courses.

Indifference is important to understand. Do you just say that you are indifferent when in reality you care? Is it a buffer so that your stepchildren don't disappoint you?

As a stepmother, it seems to me that real indifference is hard to sustain over a long period; it implies complete lack of involvement. That's very difficult when the person you love is so deeply tied to his children. Indifferent behavior over the long-term will not be taken well by your partner. It closes the door for his desire to share that part of himself with you — and thus also closes the door to real openness between you.

That basically leaves you with the last alternative: You can be kind. If you have your own children, you are well aware that, as a biological parent, you often catch yourself making excuses for your own child's behavior. You will certainly forgive and at least try to understand. Realize then, that this is what your husband feels toward his children. If closeness is what you are striving for, then you must at least make the effort to be tolerant and that takes compassion and kindness.

In *Compassion and Self-Hate*, Rubin describes several levels of caring, placing *real kindness* at the pinnacle of the caring ladder. He interprets real kindness as *active caring*. Next on the rung is *passive caring* which is also good. Indifference is less so, although not so destructive as cruelty, which ranks at the bottom. Passive caring is an offshoot of real kindness, which requires the energy of action (as does real love). Real kindness means we must be willing to sacrifice our needs at times for another's. Rubin does not imply that we should be martyrs or doormats; rather, he refers to the sort of *deep caring* which propels us to make sacrifices without feeling cheated or resentful. A mother putting her child through college, at great expense to herself, is a strong example of deep caring.

Obviously as a stepmother you do not need to go to this length to show active caring. However, you may demonstrate kindness (active caring) by sacrificing some of your priorities for the benefit of your husband and his children. Helping him celebrate his son's birthday, instead of going to your bridge group (which you might prefer to do), is one example.

If you feel that this is not within you to give or in the past you have demonstrated indifference, then passive caring is a considerable improvement and very nice too. It is an expression of your sensitivity to others' needs and feelings. Although Rubin makes a qualitative judgment on passive caring (he feels that it requires too little expenditure of our energy to be called active support or caring), not all of us are designed to give on the active level. To my mind, sympathy, empathy and sensitivity all seem excellent reactions for stepmothers, and would no doubt be appreciated by most fathers. If you are capable of this, it qualifies you for top status among stepmothers and second wives! It certainly beats anger (repressed or otherwise) and other negative emotions.

In my role as stepmother I have vacillated over the years between active and passive caring. Let's take the emphasis off passive and active, however, and consider that in varying degrees, I and you can choose to care: first for your husband, and then for the relationship you have with his children. No one can tell you to like his children, and there is no formula for establishing a great relationship with them. Whatever depth of relationship you have now, the issue is that you committed yourself to caring about it. Stepchildren, especially older ones, may make it quite impossible for you. What matters is that you maintain your integrity to your "ideal," meaning your effort to convey, on a consistent basis, that you intend to be kind, not resentful or bitter. Hopefully, your kindness will be appreciated if not by the children then certainly by your husband. With his support, you will form a strong unit for your family, and the children will be less likely to play one of you against the other.

During periods of conflict, it might seem easier to throw in the towel and opt for indifference. Think again. These children are a part of your life, and it can only weaken the intimacy you share with your husband. Express aggression or bitterness, and it will not get better. Express hope and optimism, and it will.

You Are A Package Deal Too

Acknowledge your natural reaction first, which is "I don't need this; I didn't bargain for this." That is true. When you married, you could not have been able to predict everything you would have to face, the circumstances and attitudes that would come into play. He is a package deal. You fell in love with him, but you cannot discard what he brought with him. Just as he cannot discard what you brought with you: your religion, love for your parents, or your weakness for rich foods. He may never come to love the people you care about most, nor agree with you philosophically on those things which you consider important. But hopefully, he will be able to fully accept everything you are, for both your sakes. That's the give and take of marriage.

In reasoning out my frustrations, I needed to remind myself of this: Even though I had not brought children with me from a past marriage, I was a package deal as well. David needed to accept and understand my past hurts, my own personal history. Only my first high school love, with whom I shared four years, was the recipient of that naive freshness which each of us gives perhaps but once. That kind of purity of heart is not easy to carry forward into subsequent relationships.

A package deal is really only what we inwardly make of it. I believe it is unwise to be overly concerned just because a man has one or more relationships or marriages behind him. The crux lies more in the *emotional baggage* he may bring with him. And this is very individual. Some men, though they may have been married only once, have enough emotional baggage to equal ten wives in their past.

Although I am a believer in independence within a marriage, I don't think it benefits the relationship to live completely by the philosophy, "I'll do my thing, and you, yours" — especially within a blended family. I may decide that I need a weekend away for a "mental vacation" from my family, but I cannot and would not wish to take a mental vacation from David, his children, or even Heather, for life. When I chose to become part of a stepfamily, I also accepted the responsibility that I must pay a price along with the happiness I would experience. I chose and worked at giving trust, until I could. Finally, I was able to extend my trust openly, without reserve.

Visitation And Bad Timing

For David's children who visited their father in his household, it was important to learn that, just as life in their home had its sunny and dark periods, so our house too had a similar up-and-down emotional climate. Quite apart from our involvement with Elizabeth and Robert, David and I have had our share of problems. It has happened on numerous occasions that Elizabeth's and Robert's visits were badly timed for us as a couple. Weekends have not always fallen in line with our individual or marital needs. But what was there to do? Canceling seemed unkind. In our hearts, we did want to share time with them but did not always feel up to the task. Another consideration was Adam and Annie, who awaited Robert's, and Elizabeth's visits with excitement. A double disappointment if we cancelled.

One of my unhappiest blended family weekends illustrates the complexity of this. Elizabeth and Robert were scheduled to arrive on the same weekend not only of my 25th-year high school reunion but also of the manuscript deadline for my children's cookbook. The pressure of the deadline had taken its toll, and contributed to a very bad cold. Imagine my distress as I worried about the manuscript, my untidy house which was unprepared for the weekend, and my sickly appearance for the reunion. I had been looking forward to an "all-night sleep-over" with two long-time school mates after the Friday evening reception. What misery! I had a choice: To go to the reunion (thereby missing my deadline and breaking the contract due date) or to cancel. I cancelled and cried for hours. That weekend was a personal low for me. David's sympathy and support didn't change the fact that I was miserable.

After a full weekend in that atmosphere Elizabeth and Robert were likely relieved to get home. On happier occasions, however, David and I have sensed the reluctance in Elizabeth's and Robert's good-byes. "It's been fun, and we're sad it's Sunday" was the unspoken feeling in the air. During those times, we have felt our family to be strong and cohesive. Sad feelings have often been expressed by Adam and Annie, who find it difficult to "let go" on Sunday, and who wished Elizabeth and Robert could live with us full-time. Adam has often said he would have liked Robert to attend his school, so that he could have an older brother around to protect him. Sometimes, though, it feels to me that, of the four children, it is Elizabeth and Robert who find it most difficult. They receive "weekend doses of Dad," rather than nightly ones. But it is an adjustment they made long ago, and a reality we adults must not dwell upon.

What parents can do, however, is strive to keep the visits consistently good, facing the problems as they come along. To that end, it is a good idea to establish occasional family meetings. Small hurdles can be overcome when each family member contributes his input of feelings. Just as Annie had to learn that Elizabeth could not play "Barbies" with her for hours on end, so Elizabeth and Robert learned not to expect that each weekend was an on-going agenda of fun activities. The older children were asked to be willing to participate in some household chores; the younger ones had to accept that watching "Solid Gold" was more enjoyable for Elizabeth and Robert than "Polka Dot Door."

At the same time our children have worked through the little negative hurts, like the time when Adam felt that Robert was bossing him. These give-and-take situations are part of any family, and the welfare of each individual must be considered and understood. Like life in any large household with four or more children and possibly only one bathroom, it boils down to waiting your turn, sharing the same space, sometimes even understanding the meaning of one member's urgent priorities, and being willing to step aside to consider him first.

Stepmothers Are Taken For Granted

Even if you are a nurturing type who acquiesces to your children's needs easily, the time will still come when you question the return for your love and efforts. Should you have children of your own, you are already well aware of how much children take for granted. It seems to me that much of what children need involves consistency, along with some ritual or tradition, and above all, loving role models. If they have this from birth, they are conditioned to expect it naturally, without much fanfare, despite the fact that you as an adult need similar expressions of nurturing attention. Your passage into motherhood brought with it societal expectations of maturity and self-sacrifice. As you try to fulfill your role, you carry in your heart the hope that in years to come your children will have internalized the valuable lessons you were trying to teach them and will one day understand and appreciate all you have done on their behalf. For those of us who are stepmothers, we would prefer to receive this appreciation sooner, rather than later.

There will be times when you feel as significant as the wallpaper. I too have echoed these same feelings. "Is it my food they love or me?" I've wondered many times. I console myself with the well-known axiom, *That which you sow, that will you reap.*

Our emotional universe works on certain truths and natural laws. One of these laws is The Law of Compensation. Thus, I trust that after investing my love and energy into David's children, eventually I will visibly see that I have a good deal of credit in my "love account." Credit which will be extended to me in kind when I disappoint them or am lacking in emotional funds. And credit which will give them a willingness to develop amnesia in relation to our bad moments and choose to remember that which was good.

It is my trust in this compensatory law which helps me every year around Mother's Day, when I feel by-passed by Elizabeth and Robert. I nostalgically look at the cards written especially for women who fall into the slot of "Other Mothers," or "Just like a mother," or "A friend on Mother's Day," and yes, "Stepmothers." Any one of them would have given me the "warm fuzzies" for days.

The fact that David didn't receive a Father's Day card either seemed inconsequential; after all, David *knew* he was loved. It was my ego which craved a small sign of special recognition. A little verse gushing with sentiment does a stepmother good, now and again.

When your negative emotions take hold and you find yourself wondering how you'll ever recharge your batteries enough to begin to demonstrate caring — what then?

How To Cope

What works best for me is a combination of inspiring mental and physical activity. After a healthy period of wallowing in my feelings with music that resonates to my mood, I eventually get angry enough with myself to do something positive. First, I turn to my favorite sources of inspirational literature. Second, I take time out to give myself some additional physical nurturing. I begin a process of personal healing in which I go within myself to re-affirm my ideals and to assess whether I have maintained my integrity to these beliefs. I also need to go *without* to see myself mirrored in others. This helps me re-establish the balance between myself and those people in my life, and to understand my relationship with nature and the universe. Most importantly I focus on my journal which has always been my best tool for achieving insight into my life.

When you feel frustrated, fed up and inadequate in relation to your role as stepmother, you might try some of the methods I use to bring myself back to a more positive frame of mind.

1. Start writing in a journal.

Many frustrations can be diluted through the process of writing. But don't allow your thoughts to revolve only around negative emotions. Dwelling on the past is only useful if it helps you understand the present. Because our memories give us an incomplete picture of the past, journal writing will often facilitate the synthesis of your thoughts. It will help you draw valuable conclusions about your present situation, as well as focus on your goals and the ideals to which you aspire. *Don't* censor your writing; it has little value if you aren't honest. Denials and rationalizations will surface, and positive feelings will be mirrored back to you as well.

2. Take time to develop something which is meaningful to you spiritually.

Your inner self is your essence and needs attention. How you nurture it is individual. Yoga, backpacking in the woods, classical music, searching for wild mushrooms, meditating or praying, are all examples of private ways we energize ourselves from within.

3. Learn the art of mental imagery.

Read Shakti Gawain's book, *Creative Visualization*. Then, soak in the bathtub and dwell on the images of warm memories you have shared with your husband and stepchildren. Relive these scenes in your mind and affirm that your relationships are now becoming more positive. I always retain a picture of Robert and me, watching an old musical together alone at midnight. He was highly amused at the way I crooned with Nelson Eddy and Jeanette McDonald in *Indian Love Call*. Although he acknowledged mild boredom, he did stay anyway. We both felt a mutual closeness as he took the opportunity to tease and I to ham it up.

4. Retreat from your family for a time.

It helps to distance yourself on occasion. When you're not in the mood to analyze or socialize, doing something mindless often works well for me, especially when I'm angry. By the time I have wandered around a shopping center for a number of hours, my negative feelings have been diluted. If you realize this form of escape is what you need, don't let yourself be persuaded to take along a child who loves to shop. I have sometimes choked out a *no* with great difficulty when Elizabeth asked to come along on my long walk or shopping trip. It bothered me not to include her, but I needed the space. One caution: If you are a compulsive shopper or impulse buyer, don't go shopping when you are low. It will make you feel worse. Go to the park or a museum instead.

5. Talk to a best friend who sincerely cares about giving you positive and honest feedback.

Think about who you turn to. You may have a friend who is a wonderful person, but has a pessimistic reaction to life. That's not what you need when you are down. Don't indulge in a post-mortem of your negative experiences. Instead, use your friend as a sounding board to help you gain insight into how you can make your relationships better.

My own experiences have taught me that relatives are not always the best to turn to for advice. Although they may be of help and empathize with you in the moment, they will probably also worry about you long after the crisis has passed. Anxious looks from parents are hard to take the next time you are with them. There are times when I have made negative remarks about David to my parents and later, when they expressed the same criticism, I found myself staunchly defending him. Don't forget that your parents are biased in their sympathy.

Confiding in your in-laws may be an even more unwise choice. If your relationship is good, they will react as parents. If not, their loyalties lie with their son and you may come to represent what they interpret as his problem.

6. Talk to your husband alone.

If he is a receptive person, he will try and work through your feelings with you. Possibly he has a solution. If his approach is not helpful, it is still a good idea to let him know what is bothering you; otherwise, he will be trying to second-guess you. Don't expect your husband to understand all your feelings; he is too close to you and at the same time is influenced by his own emotions.

7. Take a positive parenting course.

Many things were clarified for me when I took a course in Adlerian Psychology. From this experience, I came to understand that teenagers have but two primary goals: They seek excitement and they seek freedom. Since our household offered neither of these to Elizabeth and Robert, I instantly understood why they seemed less interested in visiting us as they grew older.

I also achieved much insight into the power struggles I was having with Adam and Annie and began to use the method of "logical consequences" in improving their behavior. The Adlerian Psychology course I attended also taught me how to deal with my feelings of discouragement. I was advised to try to think about what I would do if they were not mine, then to act on that feeling. I know that I often treated Elizabeth and Robert with more objectivity than my own children.

8. Accept that as a stepmother, you are a non-parent.

The minute you expect all of your ideas to be accepted, you set yourself up for disappointment. These children are not yours to mold but only to influence. You cannot expect them to absorb your beliefs and values when they express, in part, the beliefs of their mother. Give them the gift of your sense of humor, creative abilities and caring.

9. Keep your role as nurturer in its context.

You are more than your family. See yourself as the sum of all your parts: career, personality, feelings, values, strengths, appearance, knowledge, and your relationships.

I have discovered that excessive nurturing was my neat little distraction for avoiding growth in other areas of my life. When I took the focus away from family, what was there to focus on? I had to face the fear of risk. To direct my thoughts elsewhere meant I would also have to risk displeasing those people in my family who did not want me to change. Whenever I reached a point of frustration with my blended family, I found that I had failed to follow my intuition somewhere along the way and had put my needs secondary to theirs too often. To risk change meant that I had to develop self-trust as well as learn to listen to my intuitive voice.

10. Acknowledge your personal power.

On some level, you feel powerless as a stepmother. Personal power is the knowledge that your love, as well as your decisions, is based on personal free choice. Ruth Ross, author of *Prospering Woman*, defines personal power as separate from that which we gain or manifest in our world. It is a quality of inner strength which makes us more than just appear to be strong or powerful. Developing personal power requires not only self-approval, but also a feeling of self-worth. Without these you will be unable to approve of yourself, and you will be vulnerable to the approval (or blame) of others. The key to personal power is to take responsibility for your life as you have worked to create it, and also to know that you have it within you to create positive change.

11. Understand the concept of internal motivation.

I believe that most of the time we get exactly what we want. We may think we want something on a conscious level, but if we haven't achieved it, perhaps on a deeper level, we also haven't really wanted it enough and have blocked the goal. Decide on your goals and assess how internally motivated you are in achieving them. You must truly desire something on a deep level if you are to succeed. Whether it is your desire for more emotional intimacy or to write poetry, you must then follow up with action.

Making change requires three things on your part: *commitment, discipline* and *willingness*. Without the willingness to accept a different attitude or pattern of behavior, the probability of success is greatly diminished. Together with willingness, you must internalize a real *commitment*, one which is born of a deep emotional desire to change.

Often this gut-level desire does not come until we have hit bottom emotionally, and experienced true despair. *Discipline* is the only way you can change deeply-entrenched modes of thinking and behavior. Affirmations are a way to discipline your mind.

12. *Stop judging yourself and others.*

Don't let yourself become a *watchful Argus*. Expectations imposed by self or others will only set you up for feelings of failure. Dispose of the inner score card on which you tally your ability to be super-woman or super-stepmother. Perfection should not be one of your goals. And don't paralyze yourself with over-analysis in which your actions are judged in terms of right and wrong. You did the best you could.

Focus also on the good in your family by seeing the glass always half full, not half empty.

Conclusion

Ve get too soon oldt, and too late schmardt.

Anonymous

This amusing home truth is inscribed on a wooden plaque I gave to my father some time ago. It suits us both, as I have often exaggerated his German accent.

Of the "schmardts" which I have acquired with age, the most valuable are lessons which I have garnered from my experiences within my parental home and blended family. Together with a need for growth within my spiritual and creative self, all that essentially remains important is family. They are a part of my core from which all other things flow and harmonize.

Each of us yearns for the genuine support of our families. To those individuals who say this does not matter, my response is that this attitude is born from irreconcilable past hurts. On a much deeper level, family *always* matters. We need to be understood, particularly by those who have participated in our development.

Humorists have been parodying what they think is the typical Jewish mother for years. "After all I did for you" is a well-worn phrase, used to remind children of the sacrifices made in the name of love. The disillusionment is felt because the expected return, for the many exhausting hours of energy, is not forthcoming. Parents, who feel that they don't matter enough to their children, have chosen to dwell on the sacrifices, rather than the love which motivated these sacrifices in the first place.

If loving and giving had no price (one which must be willingly paid to be real), then everyone would be doing it. Learning the responsibility of love has been one of my major lessons in life. The commitment I made to my stepfamily facilitated its growth. As I invested my time and energy, my commitment strengthened proportionately. But it was the working through of my mistakes, and the pain of dealing with them honestly, which brought me to a true understanding of the responsibility of love and its price. My relationships in the blended family were my teachers. And in learning my lessons, my love was tested when I was required to sometimes put these relationships ahead of my own ego needs. In the time when it was right to do so, I discovered that I need not sacrifice my values, my very identity or essence in the process. It was possible to find personal fulfillment within the framework of my blended family.

The give and take of family love will always remain a challenge. When a family lives in close proximity (physically or emotionally), there is a great temptation for each to influence, alter or judge the other. Why is this? Because a family is a many-faceted mirror in which we see ourselves. The opinions and values which are expressed by others reflect back on us and make us question our own. If these values differ, we desire to persuade others to see as *we* see, to prove to ourselves that *our way* is right. If we stand alone in our views, we must "back ourselves up" to family and the world — and that is not always easy.

Our need to find strength in numbers is demonstrated each time a family member voices a negative opinion to another within the safety of the family circle; otherwise, one-on-one, he might not have found the courage. What he looks for in doing this is not only a "back-up" for his point of view, but the validation that this view is right.

If we are to achieve a level of nonjudgment within our families, we must become less concerned with who does or does not live as we do, or who agrees or disagrees with us. What is most important is that we feel genuine respect for one another. Furthermore, we must be completely aware of our own values and be willing to passively back them up in the presence of our family. By "passive," I mean without taking a defensive posture, and we must be willing to accept the attitudes of others. This approach is only possible if we possess an inner knowledge and respect for ourselves. Once we have this, should our family disagree with us, we can "live with it." From my standpoint, the times when I have experienced the deepest sadness or hurt within family is when I have felt that I as a person have not been given the respect I deserve.

When this happens, as I am sure it has to each of us at one time or another, we have but two choices: continue to love and respect those who have hurt us, or pull away emotionally and/or cease our interaction with them. I do not believe that the latter is a fulfilling solution in the long run. It will only serve to create loneliness and isolation. This is the polar opposite of the positive feelings of individuality and separateness we experience when we give and receive real love.

My life in the blended family has given me deep and satisfying ties. In the times when I am disillusioned, what sustains me is the belief that our lives are renewable from moment to moment. I try not to dwell on guilt, but rather to focus on a trust which tells me that we are all doing the best we can.

What real answers are there in learning to love within the blended family? If, as the song goes, *There ain't no cure for love*, I am ultimately left with the question of how I choose to see the experience. In this regard, the English philosopher William James has influenced my attitudes most. In his writings, he teaches that you can change your life and also your experience by changing your thoughts. This requires repetitive affirmations in order to internalize new attitudes. Our thoughts are a magnetic force field, which attracts that which we think. Our reality is the manifestation of all our thoughts. Ask yourself then, *Is it love itself which makes you happy, or are you happy because you love?*

If, as Marcel Proust writes, *The real voyage of discovery consists not in seeking new landscapes, but in having new eyes,* then this is possibly the only cure for love. In the process of my personal journey in search of love in the blended family, I also discovered "new eyes."

Postscript

A Motherhood Initiate

Oh pregnancy — oh holy state
Although I did procrastinate
And waited until 28
To find myself a willing mate
With whom I could collaborate
Someone who I could liberate
Or should I say, domesticate
I qualify; make no mistake
I do not mean subordinate

In retrospect, I must relate
I still cannot appreciate
Nor did I ever radiate
A *glow* whilst in the pregnant state

Perhaps because I overate
Gained 40 pounds of excess weight
Was prone to sleep and vegetate
Completely disproportionate
I had to circumnavigate
Myself through all the subway gates

What really did infuriate
Were friends who would pontificate
And otherwise exaggerate
Their own childbirths to illustrate
Until my heart would palpitate

And God forbid I should berate
My mother who is very "straight"
And still feels we should segregate
All husbands on delivery dates
Not meaning to discriminate
She claims men are too delicate

At last, the long-awaited date
My labor pains began at eight
With little time left to debate
My doctor would evaluate
If I'd begun to dilate

Baby began to agitate
Contractions did accelerate
I wish I'd had a surrogate!

With no choice now to speculate
I had to breathe and concentrate
I barely could articulate
For fear I'd hyperventilate

Imagine then, how jubilate
I felt, when I first held my Kate

Angela Neumann Clubb

Bibliography

The Association for the Advancement of Psychiatry Committee. **The Joys and Sorrows of Parenthood.** New York: Scribner, 1973.

Baker, Nancy. **New Lives for Former Wives.** New York: Anchor Press/Doubleday, 1980.

Baruch, Grace, Rosind Barnett and Caryl Rivers. **Lifeprints.** New York: McGraw-Hill Book Co., 1983.

Berger, Dr. Stuart. **Divorce Without Victims.** Boston: Houghton Mifflin, 1983.

Berke, Grant. **Games Divorced People Play.** New Jersey: Prentice-Hall, 1981.

Chernick, Dr. Beryl and Dr. Noam Chernick. **In Touch: Putting Sex Back Into Love and Marriage.** Toronto: Signet Books, 1979.

Francke, Linda Bird. **Growing Up Divorced.** New York: Fawcett Crest, 1983.

Frydenger, Tom and Adrienne. **The Blended Family.** Michigan: Chosen Books, 1984.

Gaylin, Dr. Willard. **Feelings.** New York: Harper & Row Publishers, 1979.

Gettleman, Susan and Janet Markowitz. **The Courage to Divorce.** New York: Simon & Schuster, 1974.

Getzoff, Ann and Carolyn McClenahan. **Stepkids: A Survival Guide for Teenagers in Stepfamilies.** New York: Walker and Company, 1984.

Jolin, Peter G. **How to Succeed as a Stepparent.** New York: Signet Books, 1981.

Kome, Penny. **Somebody Has To Do It.** Toronto: McClelland & Stewart, 1982.

Paris, Erna. **Stepfamilies: Making Them Work.** New York: Avon Books, 1984.

Peck, Dr. Scott M. **The Road Less Traveled.** New York: Simon & Schuster, 1978.

Rowlands, Peter. **A Book for Separated Families.** New York: Continuum Publishers, 1982.

Rubin, Dr. Theodore Isaac. **Compassion and Self-Hate.** New York: Ballantine Books, 1975.

— **One on One.** New York: Viking Press, 1983.

Salk, Dr. Lee. **What Every Child Would Like His Parents To Know about Divorce.** New York: Warner Books, 1973.

Steinem, Gloria. **Outrageous Acts and Everyday Rebellions.** New York: Holt, Rinehart and Winston, 1983.

Walker, Glynnis. **Second Wife, Second Best.** Toronto: Paperjacks/Doubleday, 1985.

Wallerstein, Judith S. and Joan Berlin Kelly. **Surviving the Breakup: How Parents and Children Cope with Divorce.** New York: Basic Books, 1980.

Winston, Sandra. **The Entrepreneurial Woman.** New York: Newsweek Books, 1979.

Further Suggested Reading

Anderson, Nancy. **Work With Passion.** New York: Carroll & Graf Publishers, Inc., 1984.

A book which closes the barriers between work and play and helps you explore and utilize your creative gifts in work which gives you joy.

Gawain, Shakti. **Creative Visualization.** California: Whatever Publishing Inc., 1978.

A New Age classic on the philosophy and method of mental imagery to visualize desired goals with guided meditations to help you get in touch with your "higher self." Note: Companion tapes are also available from the publisher.

Gawain, Shakti. **Living in the Light.** California: Whatever Publishing Inc., 1982.

A valuable sequel to *Creative Visualization* with special focus on your relationships and how each "mirrors" and teaches you some aspect of yourself.

Goldsmith, Joel S. **Our Spiritual Resources.** New York: Harper & Row Publishers, 1978.

This renowned spiritual lecturer has authored numerous books, all of which will inspire you to contemplate the nature of meditation, prayer, material concerns and love.

Procaccini, Dr. Joseph and Mark W. Kiefaber. **Parent Burn-out.** New York: Doubleday & Co., 1983.

Who is vulnerable to burn-out, how it affects the quality of family life and a step-by-step guide to recovery. Essential reading for anyone experiencing emotional fatigue with parenting or stepparenting.

Ross, Dr. Ruth. **Prospering Women.** California: Whatever Publishing Inc., 1982.

An inspirational book intended to replace limited, negative thinking with a "prosperity consciousness." Exercises are included for insight and self-examination. Note: Companion tape is also available from the publisher.

Sheehy, Gail. **Passages.** New York: Bantam Books, 1980.

> **For anyone in a life transition, Sheehy explains some of the predictable inner emotional shifts which take place in men and women, and the disparity between them, as they struggle to adjust to the next "passage."**

Viorst, Judith. **Necessary Losses.** New York: Ballantine Books, 1986.

> **Viorst combines her knowledge of psychology and life and writes about numerous painful experiences of loss, and positive growth which comes from it.**

Wylie, Betty Jane. **All in the Family.** Toronto: Key Porter Books, 1988.

> **A book to help you understand yourself and others. Important information and insight into various stresses experienced by individuals, couples and families.**

Ywahoo, Dhyani. **Voices of Our Ancestors.** Boston: Shambhala Publications Inc., 1987.

> **Native spirituality and ritual, with emphasis on the need for the development of a "caretaker consciousness" in today's world. This book inspires a sense of "world family" and community fellowship.**

Glossary

Active speaker/
Listener partnership

An equal distribution of "voice" in a relationship in which partners willingly interchange roles and practice good speaking and listening with one another.

Affirmation

A strong, positive statement used in inner dialogue which "affirms" that a wished-for outcome or goal is already so; the purpose is to recondition our minds to displace old negative beliefs with new, positive beliefs.

Back-door honesty

Anger which is masked by honesty when an unpleasant truth is told in the guise of "doing good" but for the purpose of lashing out against another person.

187

Breaking the mold

A term coined by Susan Gettleman and Janet Markowitz, authors of *The Courage to Divorce*, to describe the rejection of traditional attitudes and behavior patterns which were once accepted regarding separation and divorce.

Cooperation/ Competition conflict

The natural desire to compare and compete, opposing an equal willingness to cooperate, creating a feeling of inner conflict and anxiety.

Creative visualization

A technique of mental imagery, used positively, in which a desired goal is repetitively focused upon in meditation and through written and spoken affirmations of intentions or wishes.

Dirt cycle

A coined term to describe the never-ending and ungratifying task of housecleaning which creates feelings of frustration and lack of accomplishment in many women.

Life passage

A predictable phase or crisis which occurs in men and women, creating an emotional shift and re-evaluation of values and patterns of behavior and the adoption of new beliefs.

The marriage myth	A coined term to describe societal conditioning which insists that marriage is "forever" and "all-encompassing" in which partners can expect to fulfill all roles and needs for one another.
Mastery and pleasure	Terms coined by the authors of *Lifeprints* to describe the balancing of two components of self, which allow one to achieve satisfaction and self-esteem from fulfilling work (mastery) and feelings of contentment from marriage, children and sexuality (pleasure).
Out-of-step anxiety	A coined term by the authors of *Lifeprints* to describe the societal belief that a woman "should" stay home with her children if she is economically able to and the anxiety this creates for her if she enjoys working and wishes to step out of line.
Personal power	The quality of inner strength which can be developed by focusing on feelings of self-approval and worth and our willingness to change core beliefs and accept responsibility for our actions.
The pipeline	The continual back-and-forth flow of tales and information within families and stepfamilies.

Psychological autopsy   A term coined by Nancy
Baker, author of *New Lives for
Former Wives*, suggesting the
need to re-analyze the
marriage to determine if it
still "works" and whether
the marriage has been
"outgrown."

Reconciliation fantasy   A secret wish harbored by
children of separation or
divorce that their parents will
reconcile or remarry. This
fantasy is often carried over
after one parent has
remarried.

Repressed anger   Anger which is not ventilated
or communicated openly but
which is suppressed and
directed inwardly, creating
other destructive emotions
such as self-hate, guilt,
recrimination or sabotage.

Role strain   The attempt to juggle and
fulfill several roles at once
(wife, mother and career
woman), creating physical
and emotional pressures
which can result in strain
and imbalance.

Sibling rivalry   The cooperation/competition
conflict between siblings or
stepsiblings in a family.

Unfinished business   Unresolved issues and
feelings which need to be
dealt with and resolved on
both external and internal

levels after separation and
divorce.

Unhooking The process of mental,
emotional and physical
detachment from one's mate,
taking approximately two
years.

Unspoken agreements The private terms within
a relationship concerning
issues or tasks which
may not necessarily be
verbalized but have been
communicated from the
onset by behavior or an
unspoken understanding.

About The Author

Angela Neumann Clubb graduated in English and German Literature from the University of Western Ontario in 1972. After gaining experience in sales and public relations, she established herself as a counselor and workshop facilitator in the fields of career and self-motivation. During the period as a stay-at-home mother, Angela's writing career was launched with the publication of *Mad About Muffins* in 1982 (the first of her three cookbooks). Her speaking in food shows, in which Angela incorporated anecdotes about her stepfamily, was the genesis of *Love In The Blended Family* and her career as a motivational speaker in family and women's issues. She further developed her counseling skills through study at the Adlerian Institute of Toronto. This book is the result of a long period of self-study and learning, affirming Angela's enthusiastic, thoughtful approach to life. She lives in Burlington, Ontario, with her family.

YOU CAN SUCCEED!

With Changes Magazine — America's Leading Recovery Publication

Receive A Free Issue Now!

Discover the magazine that's giving thousands of people across the United States the vital self-healing tools they need to reach their personal recovery potential.

Each copy of Changes brings you new information on today's recovery issues like self-esteem, sexuality, co-dependency, relationships, and the inner child. Plus you'll receive news on support groups, innovative recovery techniques, and insights from featured personalities like Oprah Winfrey, John Bradshaw, and Leo Buscaglia.

TAKE THIS SPECIAL OPPORTUNITY TO RECEIVE A FREE ISSUE OF CHANGES
BY RETURNING THE COUPON BELOW.

Yes, please send me my free issue of **Changes** Magazine — a $3.75 newsstand value! If I decide to subscribe, I'll pay your invoice for $18.00 for a one-year subscription (6 issues including my complimentary issue) and save 20% off the newsstand price. If I don't choose to subscribe, I'll simply write "Cancel" on the invoice, return it to you, and owe nothing.

Name _____
(please print)

Address _____ Apt. _____

City _____ State _____ Zip_____
FCCHG1

☐ Please add my name to your mailing list for advance notice of conferences in my area plus catalogs of recovery books, audio tapes, and special gifts.

SEND TO: The U.S. Journal Inc.
            Subscriptions
            3201 SW 15th St.
            Deerfield Beach, FL 33442-8190